YORK NOTES

General Editors: Professor A.N. Je̶
of Stirling) & Professor Suheil Busʰ̶
University of Beirut)

Daniel Defoe

MOLL FLANDERS

Notes by Lance St John Butler

MA (CAMBRIDGE)
Lecturer in English Studies, University of Stirling

**LONGMAN
YORK PRESS**

YORK PRESS
Immeuble Esseily, Place Riad Solh, Beirut.

LONGMAN GROUP UK LIMITED
Longman House, Burnt Mill, Harlow,
Essex CM20 2JE, England
Associated companies, branches and representatives
throughout the world

First published 1982
Fifth impression 1992

ISBN 0-582-03757-3

Produced by Longman Group (FE) Ltd.
Printed in Hong Kong

Contents

Part 1: Introduction   *page* 5

  Daniel Defoe's life   5

  The Augustan age   7

  Dissent   8

  A note on the text   10

Part 2: Summaries   11

  A general summary   11

  Detailed summaries   12

Part 3: Commentary   35

  Moll's isolation   35

  Life as a market   36

  Moll's morality   39

  Defoe's imagery   42

  Defoe's narration   43

  Defoe's world: the law, cruelty, money and society   45

Part 4: Hints for study   49

  Points for detailed study   49

  Selection of quotations   51

  Answering questions on *Moll Flanders*   52

  Specimen questions on *Moll Flanders*   53

Part 5: Suggestions for further reading   58

The author of these notes   59

Part 1

Introduction

Daniel Defoe's life

Defoe lived from 1660 to 1731. He was the least socially-elevated member of the group of writers who constituted the 'Augustan' age in English literature (see pp.7–8), having been born the son of a butcher in London. He lived all his life in the shadow of the political events of his day. As a young man he joined in Monmouth's Rebellion of 1685, and he was part of William III's army of invasion in 1688. From this it is evident that he was an ardent Protestant (Monmouth and William III both aimed to overthrow the Catholic King James II; William was successful). In fact he was a Dissenter (Protestant but not Anglican; Low Church; anti-Catholic; Puritan) and as such was lower in the social order than most of the famous writers of his day. Dissenters, typically, were lower-middle-class and urban: London butchers for instance. This background should be born in mind by the reader of *Moll Flanders* (see section on Dissent, pp.8–10).

In 1701 and 1702 Defoe made a literary name for himself with a poem in defence of the (foreign) King William III, called 'The True-born Englishman', and a pamphlet entitled 'The Shortest Way with Dissenters' in which he ironically advocated that the best way to eliminate Dissent would be something like a massacre. For this piece of political impudence he was imprisoned, but it marked the start of a literary career which, continuing unabated until his death, was astonishingly vigorous and prolific. Depending on what is counted as a separate title, the total number of Defoe's works can be put at 250 or up to 400 different pieces. These include poems, historical works, letters, advice, topography, travel, and political pamphlets, as well as the novels for which he is now chiefly remembered.

Besides his writing, Defoe worked as a kind of undercover agent, gathering information and spreading rumours, for various ministers of the Crown, mostly in Scotland. The early years of the eighteenth century were politically very tense, with a constant threat of Jacobite (Stuart, Catholic) rebellion, especially from Scotland. This threat became a reality with the abortive Jacobite risings of 1715 and 1745. Meanwhile the London government was bent on a union of the Scottish and English parliaments, an object which was attained in 1707. Defoe was a small but active part of the political machinery of this period.

Partly for political reasons he wrote journals—as did Joseph Addison (1672–1719), Richard Steele (1672–1729), and Henry Fielding (1707–54), to mention only a few—and numerous pamphlets. This apprenticeship in journalism gave rise to Defoe's highly realistic and down-to-earth approach to fiction. Indeed, the boundary line between factual reporting and fictional creation is often hard to draw in his work. In 1706 he wrote a *True Relation of the Apparition of one Mrs Veal* which was based on a contemporary account of real events, but which was not altogether 'true' in as much as Defoe fabricated some of the evidence and presented the facts in his own way, for the purpose of writing an entertaining pamphlet. As in our own day, fact and fiction were intertwined. Readers of *Moll Flanders* will at once remember the lengths Defoe goes to convince us that Moll's tale is genuine. There is no doubt that the novel is a patchwork of stories, more or less true, that emerged from the criminal world. So, although *Moll Flanders* is clearly fiction (a *story*, not a history), it is very close to reality in detail.

Similarly, Defoe's most famous work, *Robinson Crusoe* (1719), was presented as a true account, and it is based quite closely on the account of a shipwrecked Scots sailor, Alexander Selkirk. But the novel, for all its brilliantly realistic detail, is a construction of Defoe's own imagination. In particular—and this is what enables us to claim Defoe as the first novelist—he dramatises Crusoe's thoughts and feelings on the island in a way which, although it feels very real, can only be imaginary.

Robinson Crusoe was a great success and Defoe cashed in on it, first by publishing two sequels (*Further Adventures of Robinson Crusoe* and *Serious Reflections of Robinson Crusoe*) and then by producing a number of other novels, of which *Moll Flanders* (1722) is the best known. The full titles of some of the others are revealing: *The Life and Adventures of Duncan Campbell* (1720); *The Life, Adventures and Piracies of the Famous Captain Singleton* (1720); *The History of Colonel Jack* (1722). Here we see a claim implied that the stories are true ('Life', 'History') as, indeed, they are in parts, together with the honest tradesman's display of his wares: adventure, piracy, military life.

Later in his life Defoe turned away from fiction and went back to the hard realities which he seems to have preferred. Among numerous other publications we find books and pamphlets about servants, street robberies, and marriage, as well as such significant titles as *The Way to Make London the most Flourishing City in the Universe*, *A Plan of English Commerce*, and *The Complete English Tradesman*.

Further details of Defoe's life may be found in some of the books listed in Part 5 of these Notes. However, the details of his life, which require a knowledge of the complicated political issues of his time, do not shed as much light on his work as more general considerations about the social and intellectual climate of the period in which he lived.

The Augustan age

In 1660 when the Stuart dynasty was restored to the British throne in the person of Charles II, a new quality seemed to enter English life and letters. After the Puritanism of the Cromwellian period, a sense of liberation took hold of some of the upper levels of society and at the same time an increased admiration for things classical was felt. The years from 1660 to about 1750 are sometimes called the 'Augustan' age after the Roman emperor Augustus, of whom it was said that he found Rome brick and left it marble. His age was associated with high culture, polish, civilisation; it was the true time of classical harmony. Britain in the early eighteenth century showed some of these same characteristics: it was the period of the great neo-classical country houses, of fine clothes and manners, of the music of Handel (1685–1759, lived in England for last forty-seven years of his life) and of an urbane and cultured literature. It is worth remembering that this was the age of Louis XIV in France (died 1715).

In literature we can point to the great success of Alexander Pope's translations of Homer (1715–26) or to Lord Rochester's imitation of the Roman poet Juvenal (in his *Satire Against Mankind* of 1675) or to John Dryden's tragedy *All for Love* of 1678, a 'classicisation' of the story of Antony and Cleopatra, as examples of the high Augustan style, with its conscious imitation of Greek and Latin forms. Even Henry Fielding's *Tom Jones* of 1749 is arranged structurally according to the pattern of the classical epic and, ironically, the great Puritan John Milton (1608–74) published his highly classical epic *Paradise Lost* in the 1660s.

As the mention of *Tom Jones* may have hinted, however, this high style was not the only one available to the Augustans. Like some of the Greek and Latin authors themselves, the writers of this period indulged in vicious satire, explicitly sexual comedy, and a cheerful treatment of the roughest and lowest aspects of human life. Pope, for instance (following Dryden) developed, in a highly polished style, a technique of violent insult which has never been bettered; and in his late, great work in which he attacked all his enemies at once (*The Dunciad* of 1728, expanded in 1742 and 1743) he contrived in a grand classical form to include such unelevated content as a description of some writers diving into a ditch—part stream, part sewer—to see who could become the vilest. Similarly, Jonathan Swift (1667–1745), though capable of the most refined classical verse and sermons, was also able to produce horrifically-detailed physical descriptions (as in *Gulliver's Travels*) and a pamphlet proposing, ironically, that the best solution to the food shortages in Ireland was for the poor to sell their children for the rich to eat; he included recipes. As a final example (though there are many others) we could consider the theatre of the day. The tragedies, such as Thomas Otway's *Venice Preserv'd* of 1682 or Addison's *Cato* of 1713, are closely modelled on classical tragedy and are both serious and elevated; the comedies, however, from those of William Wycherley (1640–1716) and George Etherege (1634–91) in the 1670s to those of Henry Fielding in the 1730s tend to be bawdy, wild and farcical.

Defoe is outside nearly all this. As a Dissenter he is antagonistic to the theatre; as a lower-middle-class Londoner he is without the extensive classical education that underlies the literature of the day; he is not particularly successful as a poet; as a hard-headed realist he has no time or room for romance or elevated notions. In all the other writers of the period we can feel a tension between the high and the low, as exemplified above. When Fielding, in *Tom Jones*, wants to describe a hilarious battle between groups of unwashed country-folk in a churchyard over a trivial cause, he rises to a Homeric style (that is, a style in imitation of Homer, the epic poet, lived *c*. eighth century BC) and writes as if the gods themselves were at war; when Pope wants to brand his literary enemies with one terrible epithet—'dull'—he creates a Goddess of Dullness to bury them all in darkness. There are thus two sides to most of the literature of Defoe's age; but not to the literature of Defoe.

Defoe is English, homely, practical, unlearned. His language has an exceptionally high proportion of Anglo-Saxon-based words (as opposed to French- or Latin-based ones). In this he is akin to John Bunyan (1628–88), another English Dissenter and author of *Pilgrim's Progress* (1678) one of the classics of English Puritanism. We could say that in the later seventeenth century there were several alternative cultures: that of Puritan writers such as Milton, Andrew Marvell (1621–78), Bunyan, and some lesser figures such as Richard Baxter (1615–91); and a sub-culture of pamphlets, broadsheets and other popular papers, containing accounts of murders and hangings, practical advice, and so on. Defoe belongs more to these two cultures, the Puritan and the popular, than to the 'high culture' of the Augustans themselves. There are links, however: Defoe did write some satirical verse in his earlier years (*The True-born Englishman* of 1701 reminds us of Dryden's poems of the 1680s) and his pamphlet *The Shortest Way With Dissenters* of 1702 employs the same ironic strategy as Swift's *Modest Proposal* of 1729.

Dissent

It is worth trying to understand the qualities of mind Defoe inherited as a Dissenter. From the time of the Reformation onwards (early sixteenth century) the Protestant churches could be measured on a scale that extended from near-Catholicism at one extreme, to total rejection of bishops and even priests at the other. The main Anglican church settled down during the later sixteenth century as a moderate body, not too close to Catholicism but still retaining bishops and many Catholic features. This did not satisfy the more extreme Protestant section of English society, and they formed a sort of religious opposition to Anglicanism (the Established Church) which went under different names during the seventeenth and eighteenth centuries. These names—which covered a number of different sects which had in common only that they had no bishops, disliked Anglicanism, and hated Rome—included Presbyterians, Puritans, Independents, Baptists, Quakers, and, later, Methodists. In general these sects (and there were dozens of smaller ones) are referred to as Nonconformists (because they did not conform to the Anglican orthodoxy) or Dissenters (because they dissented from the main religion of the land). The history of England between the Reformation and the eighteenth century was at least partly influenced by the question of the status of these Nonconformists. Different kings and queens tried to solve the problem by insisting that they attend Anglican churches or by decreeing that they could do as they liked. The reigns of Charles II (1660–85) and James II (1685–8) were particularly marked by controversy and even violence on this subject.

To a student of Defoe this historical background does not matter as much as the qualities he possessed as a Dissenter. Dissent was strong in the towns, the country tending to provide no alternative to the squires' Anglicanism. The towns, notably London and Bristol, were mercantile, middle-class, and cut off from the higher levels of society. The aristocracy and landed gentry, largely Anglican, dominated parliament, the army and navy, the universities, the government, and most public life. Dissenters were legally debarred from the throne, the universities, and government posts (as were Catholics, of course). As a result they concentrated on the areas where they could succeed, notably on trade. There is a sense of making good in spite of public disapproval about the Dissenters of Defoe's period which is reflected in his novels: Robinson Crusoe and Moll Flanders, in their different ways, are outcasts who must manage to get by on their wits.

In addition to this, the theology of Dissent tended to be Calvinist. This meant that its adherents were inclined to believe in the doctrine of predestination (preached by the Swiss John Calvin, 1509-64) which states that it is already known to God who will be saved, each person being therefore predestined to either heaven or hell. One result of this doctrine was that Dissenters could see themselves as 'saints', as being among the 'elect' already, and it was very hard for them not to go on and equate this divine selection with divine protection on earth: they felt that if God had chosen them, he would show it by giving them material prosperity here and now. What followed from this was a strange and unchristian linking of worldly success with virtue, almost as if the most prosperous tradesman was *also* the one God had chosen for heaven. Thus, in spite of adhering to a strict form of Christian discipline, Dissenters respected the making of money. When, in addition to the theological point, they added the moral point that hard work was obviously a virtuous activity ('the Protestant Ethic') there was an irresistible pressure on Dissenters to work hard, sell profitably the results of this virtuous labour, become rich and go to church in high satisfaction and the hope of heaven; and all this without the help of society.

For Defoe this attitude was a blessing. He himself worked hard and clearly regarded his work as a sort of commodity, to be advertised and sold as advantageously as possible. He is the first great tradesman in literature, a representation in letters of the expanding middle class, writing to sell just as his father butchered meat to sell. He knew he would get little help from society so, like Robinson Cruoe, he looked after himself. Without influential friends to fall back on he had, like Moll Flanders, to count every penny and to struggle at all times to avoid falling into that hell of poverty (the gutter, the jail) which for a Dissenter might well be the prelude to a hell of another sort.

A note on the text

Moll Flanders was first published in 1722 and has been through many editions. This study, and most page references, are based on the Everyman's Library edition, *ed.* David J. Johnson, Dent, London, 1972, and since reprinted, which is also available in paperback. The best edition (on which the Everyman edition is based) is that of Oxford University Press, published with the rest of Defoe's work in fourteen volumes, 1927–8.

In addition, some page references are given to the Penguin paperback edition, *ed.* David Blewett, Penguin Books, Harmondsworth 1989. This edition follows the original text of 1722.

Part 2

Summaries
of MOLL FLANDERS

A general summary

Moll Flanders is abandoned by her criminal mother, when she is six months old, and is brought up in Colchester on public charity. She grows up well-mannered and refined and, at the age of fourteen, she is taken to live with some well-off people in the neighbourhood. When she is seventeen she has an affair with the eldest son of her new family and is obliged to marry his younger brother, who loves her. This man, the first of her many husbands, dies after five years, and her children by him are cared for by their grandparents.

Moll's next husband is a draper who has to escape abroad because of his debts, so she is abandoned again. She then traps a third husband by pretending she is rich; they go to America together where she discovers that he is her own half-brother, and she returns to England alone.

In England she becomes the mistress of a man with a mad wife. He gives Moll up after six years when he has a religious conversion. A banker offers to marry her if he can get a divorce; but while he is waiting for this she marries another man (in Lancashire) who turns out to be as poor as she is, or poorer. She leaves him and returns to marry the banker who has by now obtained his divorce. She settles down contendedly, but he soon dies.

After a year or two she is driven by poverty to theft. She is briefly a baronet's mistress, but from now on she is basically a professional thief. She does well, though many of her 'trade' are hanged. After a long career of crime she is at last caught and imprisoned. Sentenced to death, she turns to religion and repents. This secures her a reprieve and she is 'transported' to America instead, together with her Lancashire husband whom she had met again while in prison.

In Virginia, Moll finds that her brother is still alive, so she decides to establish herself in Maryland. She visits her brother and their son. Once her brother has died she is able to bring her son and her present husband together. Their estates do well and she is at last secure. At the age of seventy, she returns to England, prosperous and pious.

Detailed summaries

There are no chapters in *Moll Flanders*, which is written as one continuous narrative. For these detailed summaries, therefore, the novel has been subdivided at a number of natural breaks in the story. These are indicated by the appropriate page numbers in the two most common editions of the book, 'Everyman' and 'Penguin' (see a note on the text, p.10).

Author's Preface (Everyman pp.1–5; Penguin pp.37–42)

Defoe defends himself against the charge of fictitiousness by trying to insist that this is a true story (which it is not), and against the charge of immorality by insisting that the aim of the book is to show a criminal and sinner truly repentant. Just how fair these protestations are is open to question; the very fact that Defoe feels the need to write this preface at all indicates a certain uneasiness on his part about his tale with its infinite variety of criminal activity.

NOTES AND GLOSSARY:

taken up of late with novels and romances . . . : the student of English literature may find this a little surprising. Most of the 'novels and romances' of the period immediately before that to which Defoe referred (1722) which still merit attention, were written by Defoe himself (*Robinson Crusoe*, 1719; *Memoirs of a Cavalier*, *Captain Singleton* and *Duncan Campbell*, all 1720; *Colonel Jack*, 1722). One Samuel Croxall, however, published a *Select Collection of Novels*, between 1720 and 1722 and, in France, 'romances' were being published steadily in the early eighteenth century. The first part of Lesage's *Gil Blas*, a picaresque narrative of low life not unrelated to *Moll Flanders*, appeared in 1715

Notice how in the first paragraph of the preface, Defoe, for all his claims to be telling fact, says the reader must 'take it just as he pleases'.

pretends: there is no suggestion of duplicity in the eighteenth-century usage of this word. It simply means 'aspires' or 'tries (to be something)'

three-score: sixty (three times 'a score'—twenty)

Notice Defoe's Puritan background. He keeps insisting that he is writing a moral book and that it is 'modestly told'. Puritans (Dissenters) were inclined to be far more worried about sin, particularly sexual sin, than the average Anglican.

end:	aim
garbled:	pruned
levity:	lightness of tone; joking
memento:	something to remind one of something else
hare-brained:	stupid

to be more present to ourselves: to be more aware of ourselves and our situations

and lets us into the parts of them: and lets us see some part of them

a whore, and a bawd: a prostitute and a pimp

a pawnbroker: a moneylender; but here, probably, a receiver of stolen goods

a child-taker: kidnapping is not only a twentieth-century crime

---

Secion 1 (Everyman pp.7–50; Penguin pp.43–102)

Moll, abandoned by her criminal mother at the age of six months and taken up by gipsies, escapes from them and is looked after by public charity in Colchester, a town in Essex not far from London. She makes a good impression, with her good manners and air of refinement, on the old woman who looks after her (and other orphans) and on some of the ladies who visit the establishment where she lives. Her resolve not to become a household servant but rather to be a 'gentlewoman' is almost fulfilled when, on the death of the old woman, she is taken in, aged fourteen, by a rich family in the neighbourhood, and lives with them more or less as an equal of their daughters. They know her as 'Mrs Betty'.

When she is seventeen, Moll (who is pretty and a little vain) starts an affair with the eldest son of the household. Meanwhile, his younger brother falls in love with her and, although she prefers the elder—who has falsely promised her marriage—she is obliged in the end to marry the younger. This young Robin, the first of Moll's many husbands, dies after five years, and the two children she has by him are taken off her hands by her husband's parents; so she is again free, but with twelve hundred pounds in her pocket.

NOTES AND GLOSSARY:

Newgate:	the main London prison of the eighteenth century
Old Bailey:	the central criminal court
depending:	outstanding

the steps and the string: the gallows

by the forfeiture of their parents: because their parents, being criminals, have had all their goods 'forfeited', that is, confiscated

felony: a serious crime under British law

Holland: (here) fine and valuable cloth
draper: a dealer in cloth
Cheapside: a street in the City of London
pleaded her belly: claimed that she was pregnant and therefore could not be hanged
respited: her punishment was delayed
called down: (here) made to submit (to her judgement)
transported to the plantations: exiled to the colonies (where crops, particularly sugar, were planted)
I had no parish to have recourse to: throughout the eighteenth century (and for much of the nineteenth) the care of paupers, orphans and the like fell to 'the parish', the unit of local government. This care cost money, which had to be provided by the parishioners, so orphans and other dependants were unpopular. Moll, being born in prison, cannot claim that she belongs to any parish. However, when Moll is taken up in Colchester by the 'parish officers', because they cannot send her anywhere else, and because 'compassion moved the magistrates of the town', she is taken care of and says she 'became one of their own' as much as if she 'had been born in the place'
Gipsies, or Egyptians: wandering people, found throughout Europe, living in tents and caravans, and believed to have come originally from Egypt
I should go in service: I should become a domestic servant. Moll is not keen on this, especially being 'a drudge to some cookmaid', that is, the lowest kitchen servant
spin worsted: make a particular type of cloth ('worsted') from wool

In reading *Moll Flanders* (and, indeed, all novels of the eighteenth and nineteenth centuries) you should understand the class distinctions of the period and what they meant. The 'gentry'—'gentlemen' and their 'ladies' or 'gentlewomen'—were basically those who did not work. Originally their incomes derived from land, although later this became less important. Gentlemen were not necessarily aristocrats (although all aristocrats were gentlemen) or very grand; but in money, manners, education, dress, and general life-style, they were clearly distinct from other classes. In Defoe's day the urban, bourgeois, middle class were becoming increasingly powerful and numerous (Defoe himself was a member of this merchant class and, typically, was a Dissenter rather than an Anglican); but it was still the gentry who dominated the social and political scene, and to marry their daughters into the landed gentry was the dream of the London merchants. Moll, of course, does not really understand all this: by 'gentlewoman' she simply means 'not a servant'. As she says: 'All I understood by being a gentlewoman, was to be able to work for myself, and get enough to keep me without going to service, whereas they meant to live great and high, and I know not what'. This question is of great significance in the novel: Moll occasionally pretends to have a private income (in effect, to be a lady—one who does not have to work) and this attracts gentlemen (genuine in one case, not in another) who wish to assure their non-working status by marrying money. Her whole life is not simply a struggle to get enough money to survive; she wants enough to establish herself in the leisured security of the upper class. At the end she achieves this: the land may be a colonial plantation, but at the age of seventy Moll is a landowner, living off an estate in comfort.

it will hardly find you in victuals: it will hardly keep you in food

I had no policy in all this: 'policy' in eighteenth-century English meant 'deceitful planning' and implied a cunning strategy, the opposite of honesty

lass: girl

Miss: Moll is surprised to be called this, which is understandable as it then implied respect—the sort of respect accorded to gentlewoman, for instance. The Mayoress adds to this by commending Moll's hand as 'a Lady's hand'

a shilling: a coin worth five pence in modern British decimal currency. It was worth twelve old pence; there were twenty shillings to one pound

washed the ladies' laced heads: washed head-dresses made of lace

a person of ill fame: a woman of bad reputation, sexually immoral

I would dabble them in water: I would rinse them

I not only found myself clothes: Moll earned enough money to pay for her own clothes

a rare housewife: an unusually good housekeeper

to jest: to joke

she huffed me: she dismissed me angrily

here I had all the advantages for my education that could be imagined: notice what these educational opportunities for women consisted of in the eighteenth century: dancing, French, writing, and music. Perhaps she should have added drawing

spinet: a small harpsichord

to learn me everything: to teach me

but that which I was too vain of was my ruin: her beauty. It makes her proud and it 'ruins' her; 'ruin', applied to women, always meant a pre-marital affair

young gentlemen of extraordinary parts: young men of great talent

levity: light-heartedness or (here) lack of concern for others

well-carriaged: Moll is complimented here on her deportment, that is, on how she walks and 'carries herself'

a-setting: trapping

Mrs Betty: the term 'Mrs', now applied only to married women, could be used for any adult female in the eighteenth century. It means 'Mistress' (female Master or Mister), from which word we also derive 'Miss', an unmarried woman

to toast her health: to drink to her beauty, in fact

the market is against our sex just now: notice the mercantile terminology here. Defoe is a sort of early Marxist who sees the economic basis of social patterns rather clearly

you are none of them that want a fortune: 'none' here means 'not one' and 'want' means 'lack'; that is, the sister *has* a fortune

all my spirits flew about my heart: in eighteenth-century medicine there were some picturesque notions about the relationship between mind and body. The 'animal spirits' were supposedly highly-refined fluids in the blood that flowed to the heart at times of excitement. 'Flew' here is an obsolete past tense of 'flow', rather than the past of 'fly'

he was, it may be, the ruder: the elder brother's 'rudeness' is not impoliteness; 'rude' in Defoe's time meant 'rough' or 'bold' and 'forceful'. Here he is being more forceful, freer, in his wooing of 'Mrs Betty'. A little later we hear that he 'offered no manner of rudeness to me, only kissed me a great while' from which it is clear what Moll means by 'rudeness'

if I could love him again: not 'another time' but 'in return'. (Notice, in the same paragraph, 'I said little to him again' where the meaning is, again, 'in reply')

discovered: revealed

guineas: a guinea was one pound and one shilling; since decimalisation of sterling it is no longer a legal unit of currency

fired his inclination: excited his passions

I . . . did not understand the drift of it: I did not understand the meaning

I had a most unbounded stock of vanity: notice the mercantile vocabulary employed by Defoe. Moll has a 'stock' of vanity, she 'casts' (calculates) what her admirer intends, but never thinks of making any 'capitulation' (conditions) for herself. Defoe seems to see love and marriage in economic terms. On the other hand it must be admitted that Moll, in sheer self-protection, has to take a mercenary view of the matter, and her thoughts as described in the paragraph which starts 'Thus I gave myself up to ruin' show how closely money is involved in this affair

memento: reminder; warning

I told the guineas over: I counted the money

correspondence: (here) contact

circumlocution: talking around the point

turnover . . . neckcloths: the eighteenth-century equivalent of a collar and tie. The point is that the elder brother makes up a story about wanting 'Betty' to visit a shop for him. She must 'haggle' (bargain) to make her visit longer

wig, hat and sword: a gentleman could not go out without these accessories

confidant: a friend to whom one tells secrets

their carriage was altered: their behaviour (towards Moll) was changed

got vent: the family has 'got wind' of the younger brother's love of Moll: that is, they have detected it

being bred to the law: notice how the younger son of a gentleman is trained in a profession. Notice also that 'breeding' in the eighteenth century usually refers to a person's upbringing, not his parentage

in a great strait: in a tight corner; 'strait' = narrow

I used always to lie with the elder sister: in Defoe's time, and later, it was common for sisters, friends, and even servants, to share beds. Men seem to have been less keen to do this than women

he was sure our correspondence had been managed with so much address: this has nothing to do with the postal service. 'Correspondence' here means 'affair' or 'relationship', whilst the word 'address' means 'cleverness' or 'efficiency'

mortifications: things to make one ashamed

presently: immediately (not 'after a while')

gallant: lover (male)

distemper: disease

squabble: quarrel

made such a rout: made so much noise

a groat: a coin worth four old pence; equivalent to 1.66 new pence

beauty's a portion: the reference here is to a 'marriage portion'—the money a woman brings with her on marriage; a dowry

wench: girl

Robin rallied and bantered: that is, he joked and teased and would not be serious

her younger son talked after such a rattling way as he did: Robin talked in such a joking and lighthearted manner. As Defoe says, he 'rattled and jested'

the brother and all his sisters together by the ears: they are in the middle of an argument

upbraiding them with their being homely: criticising them for being plain

jade: in eighteenth-century slang this word (really meaning a tired horse) could be used of a woman either affectionately (as Robin does here) or disparagingly

all my sisters' huffing: all their interference and nonsense

this stung the elder brother to the quick: it touched him closely

don't go to sham your stories off on me: don't pretend that I'm the one who did it

rant: rage, using grand words

exigence: need

a downright breach of honour: honour is a tricky concept for the modern reader. Here the meaning is clear enough: if the elder brother abandons Moll, after promising to marry her, he will be acting dishonourably; even today we talk about 'honouring a contract' in this way. Elsewhere in *Moll Flanders*, however, the word is used in more difficult ways. Generally speaking the main thing to remember is that a man's honour was his reputation for gentlemanly qualities (courage and honesty in particular) while a woman's honour was her reputation for ladylike qualities, notably chastity. A problem arises, however, when we discover that honour is not merely a matter of reputation; dishonourable behaviour is possible in private too

I . . . carried . . . respectfully to him: I behaved respectfully towards him

I have attacked her in form five times: I have proposed marriage to her

when the plot was thus . . . broke out: when the plan was discovered

grounded on his first engagement of maintaining me: based on his original promise to support me

to lay it home to me in the worst colours: to explain it to me in a way that would make it seem as bad as possible.

like a bear to the stake: reluctantly

fuddled: drunk

whether he had had any conversation with me: here, Moll means 'whether we had made love'

Secion 2 (Everyman pp.50–89; Penguin pp.102–155)

Moll now looks about for another husband and gets a draper, a trades-man who is not quite a gentleman. He inherits some money and, having spent it all in wild extravagance, escapes from his creditors and goes abroad, leaving Moll in an odd position but with five hundred pounds to her name. She spends some time voluntarily in a debtor's prison (the Mint) but then leaves to live with a widow and to look for another husband. She learns some of the difficulties of the eighteenth-century marriage market.

Defoe offers, as an aside, a story of a woman tricking a man into marrying her although he has previously rejected her as penniless. Then Moll herself, with the help of her friend, traps a husband by allowing it to be thought that she is rich. She manages to avoid a direct lie, so he is unable to blame her later, and they are happily married. When they go over to his estate in Virginia, however, she meets his old mother, whom she discovers is her *own* mother and that she is thus married to her half-brother. When she at last reveals this, as her only means of escape from an intolerable situation, her brother becomes gloomy and suicidal and at last agrees that she should go back to England.

NOTES AND GLOSSARY:

I was courted: sought as a wife

linen-draper: a tradesman who, however rich, would not be a gentleman. This distinction was most important in the eighteenth century. Moll's husbands and lovers, as we shall see, are sometimes gentlemen and some-times not. On the whole the non-gentlemen are better for her as they tend to have some money (being in trade) whereas the gentlemen, who are not prepared to work, tend to marry Moll for *her* money, real or imagined. A good marriage was almost the only way for a gentleman to enrich him-self. Notice what Moll says in the next paragraph: 'I was not averse to a tradesman; but then I would have a tradesman, for sooth, that was something of a gentleman too . . .' It is worth pondering this and the rest of the paragraph

my money, not my virtue, kept me honest: notice the overwhelming im-portance of money in the course of Moll's life

a coach-and-six: the most expensive form of transport: a carriage pulled by six horses

postilion: a servant who assisted the coachman and rode on the coach or on one of its horses. Something like a modern courier.

liveries: servants' uniforms

page: a boy servant usually employed for display only

bantering: teasing

his lordship's chaplain ... putting on a scarf: noble families had their own priests (chaplains) in the eighteenth century. For a poor scholar at Oxford this would be a good job to get. The 'scarf' was the white neckcloth worn by chaplains and other junior clergy

fop: a dandy; a vain and idle man

he broke, got into a sponging house: he went bankrupt and was taken into a kind of debtor's prison

the Mint: as we will discover almost at once when Moll herself goes there, the Mint was a kind of voluntary debtors' prison. Bankrupts would go into it or— as here—put their goods into it because, once inside, neither man nor goods could be touched by the creditors

to go quite out of my knowledge: to go away from where I was known

at the sign of the Bull: at the public house called 'The Bull'

my Lord Rochester's mistress: John Wilmot, second Earl of Rochester 1648–80), was a notorious rake and libertine at King Charles II's court. He was also an excellent poet; two lines of his are quoted a few pages on

but it is none of my talent to preach: how true is this?

I looked like one that was to lie on hand: the market is against Betty and she is going to stay 'on the shelf' as unwanted goods

huffed: (here) rushed

he was very ill beholden to his neighbours: he owed his neighbours nothing at all for their malicious gossip about him

a kind of lofty carriage: a sort of superior attitude

the sex: women

nice: generally means 'fastidious' or 'exact'

the forwarder to venture: more prepared to take risks

lottery: state lotteries started in the early eighteenth century—a useful metaphor for haphazard fortune

having but one cast for her life: women, says Moll, have only one throw of dice in the lottery of marriage—one choice and they are stuck for life, unless of course the husband dies or disappears

an old maid: unmarried woman beyond the marriageable age

all which I had allowed to my character: all of which people admitted me to be

to change my station: to alter my position in the world (particularly from the point of view of class)

if he balked: if he hesitated

the sash in my chamber: the window in my bedroom

laid down the cudgels: declared peace

portion: dowry

I had him fast: I had caught him securely

when I should come to own my circumstances to him: when I should explain my circumstances

he was very well to pass in the world: he was well-off financially

three plantations which he had in Virginia: most of the original states of the United States of America, including Virginia, were British colonies until 1776. These colonies were mostly 'plantations' (where such things as tobacco and sugar were planted and grown) and many of these plantations were owned by people living in Britain. It was a smart thing for a British gentleman to own land in the colonies, but the people who actually lived there were often convicts and slaves

had I discovered: had I revealed

as a composition for a debt of £600, being little more than five shillings in the pound: when a man is declared bankrupt his creditors meet and agree to a 'composition' whereby his remaining assets are divided up proportionally and each creditor receives the same percentage of what he is owed. Here the percentage is 25 per cent (five shillings being a quarter of one pound in pre-decimal sterling)

many a Newgate-bird becomes a great man . . . burnt in the hand: here Moll is being told about the colonies, such as Virginia, where many convicts (those from the prison of Newgate and those whose hands have been branded with the mark of the criminal) settle and rise to important positions once their 'time is out', that is, once they are set free from working as slaves. They even become judges. The 'trained bands' are the militia, the citizen's army

victuals: food

bearing his carriage: tolerating his behaviour

expostulation: objection

contemned: despised
an apoplex: a stroke or heart-attack
cold as a clod: cold as a lump of earth
rhapsodies: (here) excessive complaints
give it me under your hand: write down (the promise) and sign it
capitulations: (here) conditions
a little distempered in his head: slightly mad
a lingering consumption: tuberculosis, perhaps
I obtained a very good cargo for my coming to England: Moll arranges to take some valuable merchandise (perhaps tobacco) with her to England, to pay for her journey and to set her up once she has reached home

---

Secion 3 (Everyman pp.89–108; Penguin pp.155–182)

Moll returns to Bristol and lodges at Bath where she takes up with a well-to-do man who, being married to a mad wife, becomes a close friend of Moll's. After much protestation to the contrary, but to her relief, he at last makes her his mistress. They stay together for six years, Moll having three children of whom only the first, a boy, survives. The gentleman then falls ill and, having been taken to 'the very brink of eternity', decides to break off the affair. Much moralising is offered on this episode, combined with a careful account of how Moll extracts money from her former lover.

NOTES AND GLOSSARY:
two and thirty days: notice how long it took to cross the Atlantic in those days
Kinsale: a small port in the south-west of Ireland
sprung her mainmast: the main mast broke
Milford Haven: a port in south-west Wales
Bristol: the principal port of south-west England
without any hope of recruit: with no hope of further help; (see, a few paragraphs further on, 'recruits of money')
Bath: a fashionable spa resort, close to Bristol
gallantry: love-affairs
I had entered into no felonious treaty: I had not started an affair with anyone
distempered in her head: mad
an advantageous character: the landlady speaks well of Moll's new admirer
but one room two pair of stairs: one room on the second floor
twelve guineas: twelve pounds and twelve shillings
he seemed distasted: he did not like

cavil: small objection

he ... did not tell it, and huddled it into the drawer again: to 'tell' is to count money; to 'huddle' is to conceal

I must housewife the money: 'to housewife' here is, strangely enough, the equivalent of 'to husband', that is, to be careful with

he obliged me to diet him: he made me provide his food. Note how Moll, and the landlady of their house, make a profit out of this arrangement; that at least is one reading of this sentence

pallet-bed: a mattress on the floor

hazarding: risking

ravisher: rapist

it is ill venturing too near the brink of a command: it is a bad thing to get too close to temptation. (Here 'command' means 'commandment' as in the 'Ten Commandments')

at our penitentials: repenting

when I grew near my time: when my pregnancy was well advanced

travail: labour; giving birth

money for a wet day: money saved against a worsening in (Moll's) fortune

a wet-nurse to tend and suckle it: a woman servant paid to feed the baby from her own breasts

Hammersmith: a suburb near London

Bloomsbury: a district of London

criminal correspondence: (here) an immoral sexual relationship

general release: here Moll means a document which she would sign and which would exonerate her lover from any further claims upon her

it is great odds but: it is extremely likely that

Secion 4 (Everyman pp.108–162; Penguin pp.182–246)

Moll's financial position is not too bad—she has four hundred and fifty pounds saved—but her social position and her long-term prospects are poor. She gets an introduction to a banker who offers to look after her money while she goes to the country where she can live more cheaply; he has a wife who lives with another man, and he offers to have Moll if he can get a divorce. When she goes to Liverpool, however, she meets a man whom she takes to be rich, and she marries him. Disillusionment soon sets in when she discovers not only that he is not rich but that he expected her to have money, which she does not. They separate, although they get on together well enough, leaving Moll to go to London where she gives birth to the result of their union—another boy. She gives her son to a poor woman, with some money to look after it, and is thus free to take up with her banker who by this time has obtained his divorce. He marries her and she settles down very happily.

NOTES AND GLOSSARY:

a goldsmith . . . broke: in the days before branch banking, people left their money with goldsmiths for safe keeping. This goldsmith goes bankrupt and his creditors receive 30 per cent of what they are owed, this being the product of the sale of his assets, in a 'composition' of thirty pounds in a hundred

I was near twenty years older: at the beginning of this section, then, Moll is forty-two years old

painting: (here) cosmetics

I was a little at a stand: I was somewhat puzzled; I didn't know what to do

cuckold: a husband whose wife is unfaithful

it stuck very close to him: it was close to his heart

you may cry her down: you can put the law on to her

he would have had me let the maid have stayed: he wanted me to tell the maid to go away and stay away

treated me: paid for me

Roman Catholics: this is an interesting passage when we consider the strong anti-Catholic feelings of the time (Catholics were excluded from the throne, parliament, the officer ranks of the army, Oxford and Cambridge and government service, for example). The question is why Defoe chooses to make this particular family Catholic, and there are two probable answers. First, he wants to show how Moll will go whichever way the wind blows—among Catholics she will seem pro-Catholic as a kind of defence mechanism. Second, as a Dissenter Defoe was in the same position as a Catholic in that he was officially condemned by the state religion of Anglicanism, so perhaps he had a certain sympathy with Catholics who suffered the same fate

to be nice in point of religion: to be fussy about religion

complaisant: (complacent) agreeable; friendly

I was here beaten out of all my measures: I was beaten at my own game; my own tricks were beaten by this big trick

West Chester . . . Ireland: Moll and her husband are near Liverpool and they are planning to get a boat to Ireland, from Holyhead

I forgot what sign it was at: Moll is talking about an inn. All such had (and still have) signs (such as 'The Bull', mentioned earlier) illustrating their names

consist with: be consistent with

equipage: coach and horses

he said he was bred a gentleman: he said that he was brought up not to work, having a certain degree of education

the putting the face of great things upon poor circumstances: concealing poverty behind a mask of riches

he was not a rake: not a playboy, not merely an irresponsible pleasure-seeker

slut: pejorative term for a woman

Dunstable: a town thirty miles north of London

some kind squabble: friendly argument

had not my effects miscarried: if my goods had not been lost

I magnified pretty much: I exaggerated

to lie in: to have a child

his process was more tedious . . . : his law-suit dragged on

I made no scuple to: I did not hesitate to

ague: (pronounced 'aig-you') an eighteenth-century name for a disease similar to malaria

miscarry: lose the child at or before birth

a midwife; but she had another calling too: that is, she was also an abortionist

I was too sensible of . . . : I was too aware of

I have given security to the parish in general to secure them from any charge from what shall come into the world under my roof: bastards (illegitimate children) and abandoned infants came under the care of the local parish officers; these people were often reluctant to accept pregnant strangers into the parish, or to encourage 'lying-in' there, because of the cost of supporting the results. Here the midwife has told 'the parish' (that is, its officers) that none of the babies she delivers will become a burden to them. (See, three pages later, where the kind lady tells Moll that her friend 'could not secure the parish')

though I want friends: although I lack friends

brazen wench of Drury Lane breeding: rude and forward girl like those of Drury Lane—referring either to the girls in the theatre there or to the prostitutes outside

burthen: burden

a child clandestinely gotten: a bastard

ladies of pleasure: prostitutes

I began to nauseate the place: she began to dislike it. 'To nauseate' is now only used in the other form: something nauseates me

got: can mean 'begotten', given birth to

it was an error of the right hand: it was a mistake in the right direction

I was brought to bed: I had a child

tattling: gossiping

not but that it was too: it was also ...

in her drolling way: teasingly, amusingly

conversation with a spirit: communication with

conscientious: Defoe plays with this word. It means 'full of conscience' (good) but it also means 'careful', which can be bad if it only means 'careful about one's own interests'

this puzzled me scurvily: this was an annoying problem. (Scurvy was an unpleasant disease caused by lack of vitamin C)

Non compos mentis: (*Latin*) mad

shagreen: a type of leather

grimace: pretence; a put-on face

a good suit of knots: clothes of a knitted material

a piece of bone-lace for a head: fine lace to form a head-dress

the minister of the parish: the local vicar or priest

a great cluster: a lot of noise

hue-and-cry: pursuit

highwaymen: roadside robbers

the mob gentry: the gang making up the 'hue-and-cry'

Secion 5 (Everyman pp.162–204; Penguin pp.246–308)

Left a widow with two children (one of whom gets forgotten, incidentally—see Everyman p.170), Moll manages to live for two years on what she inherited from her last husband, but then has to turn to theft. She leads a successful life of crime in London, indulging in street robbery and stealing from shops. Many of her accomplices are caught and hanged or transported. After a chance encounter she becomes the mistress of a baronet for about a year, but when the affair finishes she returns to theft.

NOTES AND GLOSSARY:

family: household, including servants

for five years: notice that this marriage takes Moll from forty-three to forty-eight years old

I had the vapours: I was unwell; 'the vapours' were fits of fainting and dizziness often associated with nervous disorders

Leadenhall Street: in the City of London, as are the other streets Moll mentions, such as Fenchurch Street and Billingsgate. London in the eighteenth century was still very much centred round the City, which is now only the main business section

a mercer's shop: mercers sold silk and other expensive materials

rifled: thoroughly emptied

window-board: windowsill

more money than forecast: more money than sense (to 'forecast' is to 'foretell', through wisdom perhaps)

some quilting work: sewing; this was almost the only honest profession open to women, with the depressing exception of 'service' (working as a servant)

shop-books and pocket-books: tills and wallets

I had still a cast: I still had an opportunity

to go without the circle: to go outside the circle; here the reference is to the magic circle used by witches and others when calling up the devil

purchase: Moll's word for something she can steal

a hawk's-eyed journey-man: a shop-assistant with sharp eyes

cambric: a type of cotton material

they both pleaded their bellies and were both voted quick with child: both women claimed to be pregnant (to avoid being hanged) and the judges accepted the two claims

having the brand of an old offender: this is intended literally: thieves were often branded on the thumb ('burnt in the hand') to mark them. If they were later caught stealing again they were more likely to be hanged

a circuit pardon: an amnesty

booty: stolen goods

to look narrowly into the thing: to look carefully into it

a scouring: (here) being hanged

he began to capitulate: he started to bargain

the poor boy was delivered up to the rage of the street: that is, he was beaten to death by the mob

transported: convicted criminals were often transported (to America and, later, to Australia) as an alternative to being hanged

catched: an older form of 'caught'

my Lord Mayor, and by his worship committed to Newgate: the Lord Mayor of London was, and nominally still is, the chief magistrate of that city. He is addressed as 'Your Worship'. Here he sends Moll's accomplice to Newgate, the main London prison of the period

to enter into recognisances to appear at the sessions: to undertake to appear in court

he got his indictment deferred: he had his case postponed

trifling: wasting time

to bring myself off: to get myself acquitted by the court

a piece of very good damask in a mercer's shop: damask was expensive cloth, often made of silk, sold at a mercer's, that is at a silk-shop

a lace chamber: an upstairs workshop where lace was made

I began to run a-tick again: I began to get up to my old tricks again

Bartholomew Fair: a fair held at Smithfield, in London, on 24 August each year

cloisters . . . raffling shops: these are not, of course, the cloisters of a monastery; at Bartholomew Fair there were erected rows of booths, containing shops and places of amusement (such as the raffling-shop where tickets were sold some of which won prizes); these booths looked rather like cloisters

a feather muff: a cylindrical hand-warmer, here made with feathers

full-bottom periwig: a wig with curls of hair extending down on to, and below, the shoulders. Fashionable men wore wigs between the mid-seventeenth and late-eighteenth centuries

a man heated by wine in his head, and a wicked gust in his inclination together: a man both drunk and lecherous

it would be a surfeit to them: they would have enough of it and would not do it any more

the passive jade: the unresponsive prostitute (a 'jade' was a type of horse)

I do not come to make a booty of you: I do not come to blackmail you

he alleged the wine he drank: he appealed to the fact that he had drunk some wine

he never came into a settled way of maintenance: he never set Moll up as his mistress on a regular basis

he did not keep: he did not maintain (Moll) on a regular basis

he left it off altogether without any dislike or bidding adieu: he stopped (visiting Moll) without anger and without saying a final farewell

---

Secion 6 (Everyman pp.204–236; Penguin pp.308–348)

With a cool nerve and a ready wit, Moll makes a good thing out of her 'trade' of theft. She is often nearly caught but she always escapes, and is even able to make money out of being wrongfully arrested, as she is by a milliner at one point. She is often in disguise and often scared, but she seems unable to give up her way of life. In this section Defoe takes Moll through nearly all the criminal fraternities. Eventually Moll is caught red-handed stealing some cloth and is taken to Newgate.

NOTES AND GLOSSARY:

being loath to spend upon the main stock: not wanting to touch her capital

in a very mean habit: in the clothes of someone poor

in an ordinary stuff gown: in a dress of cheap material

plate: usually means silver tableware

Indian damask: an expensive material

a laced head and ruffles: collar and cuffs of lace

huckaback linen: an expensive cloth

so many ells of Dutch holland: several feet of a type of fine cloth from Holland. (Strange, this: the cloth 'holland' could of course come from France, England or anywhere, but Defoe confusingly decides to have it come from Holland and be Dutch.) An ell was forty-five inches

a hamper of flint: not, of course, glasses made of stone; instead, a basketful of glasses made with flint-sand

when does the pitcher come safe home that goes so often to the well?: a proverb: if you use a jug often you are more likely to break it than if you use it rarely

broils: (here) embroilments; trouble

artists: (in Moll's language) thieves

mercer's journeyman: shop-assistant at the silk and cloth shop

the constable happening not to be a hired officer: in the days before a regular police force, the peace was kept by constables who were either elected from among the men of the area or hired professionals. The latter tended to be unreliable and even corrupt; the former, such as this corn-merchant, were of better sense and honesty. Shakespeare has some interesting specimens of constables in *Much Ado About Nothing* (Dogberry and Verges) and *Measure for Measure* (Elbow)

a good dab of dirt: a large lump of mud

to put myself into second mourning: particularly in the higher levels of society in the eighteenth century, it was important for widows to parade their grief. 'First mourning' ('weeds') was a suit of heavy black clothing; 'second mourning' was rather lighter and more ordinary-looking and could be put on perhaps three months after the death. There were later stages, too

mistake: note that this can be used actively in the sense of 'make a mistake'

Hick's Hall, the Old Bailey: criminal courts

pettifogging hedge solicitor: a lower-class, and probably unqualified, lawyer

he promised he would not blow the coals: he promised that he would not make things difficult (for Moll)

an accomodation: a settlement out of court

I abated his cringes: I reduced the amount he had to apologise

I was in such a plight now that I knew as ill how to behave in as ever I did in any: I was in such a difficult position that I did not know what to do; in no other case had I been more uncertain of what to do

he called one of the drawers: he summoned one of the inn servants

The Gazette: the official government publication that included descriptions of stolen property

coiners of money . . . : Moll here describes some counterfeiters, forgers of money. The punishment for this crime, especially for the person who actually 'worked the die' (operated the mould) was to be burnt at the stake

the vapours: a fit of fainting; an attack of extreme nervousness

they would have gone near to have murdered me: they would have come close to murdering me

a coming off: an acquittal

I did not close with them: I did not come to an agreement with them

privately got on shore: smuggled

this balked me: this obstructed me

a paper of lace: a small parcel of lace

the box and dice: for gambling

the gentleman who had the box threw out: he threw too high a number and lost. (The details of this dice game are not important; the main point is that Moll is careful and lucky)

tell: (here) count

not according to practice: not the custom

an old bite: a well-worn criminal trick for obtaining money

not only intolerably merry, but a little fuddled: Moll distinguishes two aspects of drunkenness: being cheerful and being confused

the Ipswich wherry: the sailing-boat bound for Ipswich (on the East coast of England). Wherries are described in the next paragraph

French pistoles . . . Dutch ducatoons . . . six-dollars: all valuable European coins of the time

two periwigs, wearing-linen . . . wash-balls: two wigs, underclothes and
shirts . . . soap
clown: country person
incognito: concealed; in disguise
rambles: country walks
he weighed the spoons: in the days of pure silver cutlery, spoons and
similar items could be weighed to ascertain their
value
saucy wenches: impertinent girls
the fatal tree: the gallows

Secion 7 (Everyman pp.236–274; Penguin pp.348–394)

In Newgate, Moll finds herself at last in the Hell she has so long expected. It is a terrible place and she becomes distracted and utterly dis-
tressed; she is obsessed with the likelihood of being hanged. After some
delays she is, indeed, sentenced to death. Under the influence of this she
at last becomes truly repentant, in which she is greatly assisted by a good
minister of religion. This man arranges to have Moll reprieved and her
sentence is at last commuted to one of transportation to the colonies.
While in prison she meets her Lancashire husband, arrested as a high-
wayman, and convinces him that the best thing is for them both to go to
America if they can. Eventually both she and her husband are able to
get on board the same ship and, using their remaining money, they
manage to obtain decent treatment and even to carry with them to
America the tools and furniture they need to set themselves up as
planters there.

NOTES AND GLOSSARY:
they flouted me with dejections: they were rude to me and put me down
my score: my bill (in the eighteenth century prisoners had to
pay for their own food and drink)
I pleaded my belly: I said that I was pregnant, in order not to be hanged
she tampered with them: she bribed them
he should forfeit his recognisance: he might lose the money he had put
up as a security guaranteeing he would appear in
court
I was as certain to be cast for my life . . . : I was as certain to be sentenced
to death . . .
gibbets and halters: gallows and nooses
the ordinary of Newgate: the chaplain of the prison
a full discovery: a full revelation. (Note the eighteenth-century sense
of 'to discover'—'to reveal to others', rather than
'to find')

I began to nauseate the man: I began to dislike him. Notice this usage of 'nauseate', meaning to dislike, rather than, as today's English, to cause someone else to dislike one

session: court

the stitch: (here) a transient pain in the side

these brave, topping gentlemen: these fine (well-dressed), first-class men

Hind, or Whitney, or the Golden Farmer: famous highwaymen of the time

a bill preferred to the grand jury: a case submitted to the High Court

my temper was touched: this word 'temper' is very useful for Defoe: it can mean 'character' or 'quality'; here it means 'disposition'

the jury found the bill for robbery: the jury found (Moll) guilty of robbery

you will be tried a-Friday: Moll has been found by the jury to be guilty; the 'trial' here is the passing of sentence by the judges

clout: (here) cloth

the very vitals: the stomach (metaphorical)

sessions-house: court-room

arraigned: formally accused

indictment: formal accusation

felony . . . burglary: these were two categories of crime, both serious. Burglary particularly involved breaking into a house to steal. Moll is, correctly, acquitted of this

bedlam: the principal lunatic asylum of eighteenth-century London

the dead warrant: the list of those who must hang

the word eternity . . . with all its incomprehensible additions: we should say 'with all its mysterious connotations'

lively impressions: vivid or strong impressions

the Recorder in my case: one of the judges

put into the carts: condemned men were taken to their place of execution in carts, to make a public spectacle of them

as a mere distemper: just like a disease. (Moll's crying is uncontrolled and involuntary)

a . . . transport . . . or passion of thankfulness: Moll feels extreme emotion; she is 'carried away' ('transported') with it

he would not have me be secure: he didn't want me to think I was safe

so ill was I beholding to fame: so poor was my reputation

flux and reflux: ebb and flow

to write down at large: to record extensively or completely

they made shift to: they managed to

the condemned hole: the part of the prison reserved for prisoners condemned to death ('death row')

he looked wishfully at me: we would say 'longingly', but Defoe's word is more expressive

taken up: given up

admitted to transportation in court: actually sentenced to be transported

this hardship broke all my measures: this problem threw out all my plans

stood very hard on: (here) pressed hard for

Deptford Reach: Moll's boat is, of course, going down the Thames

the ship weighed: the ship set sail

neither shirt or shift: a 'shift' was a nightdress or petticoat

a sea-bed . . . and all its ordinary furniture: a bunk with its sheets and blankets

mortification: shame

despicable quality: low status

three keepers of Newgate: three jailers

his chagrin at these hell-hounds: his anger at the jailers

plate: silver tableware

the great cabin: the main cabin, which was relatively comfortable, as opposed to the hold or other parts of the ship where the transported criminals were kept

mate . . . boatswain: officers of the ship

cabins built up . . . steerage: the space between the decks of an eighteenth-century ship was open: fortunate individuals could partition off small sections of it for their own cabins. The steerage was the less attractive end of the ship

to pay him by advance: we would say 'in advance'

roundhouse: (here) the captain's cabin

apply . . . to the business of the place: work hard at the business available (in America)

Secion 8 (Everyman pp.274–295; Penguin pp.394–427)

They set sail and eventually reach Virginia, where Moll sees her brother again, although he does not see her; for that reason they decide to move to Carolina. Moll discovers, however, that her mother has left her some sort of legacy which might be worth trying to collect; and also when they have sailed as far as Maryland, they find an opportunity of a good estate and decide to remain there. This estate flourishes and Moll soon finds means to go back to Virginia, where she makes herself known to her son who is delighted to find his mother again and willingly pays her the income from her mother's legacy. She does not make herself known to her brother (husband) and, conveniently, he soon dies. She is then able to explain things to her present husband and to introduce her son to him. Happiness and wealth are now assured to Moll and the book ends with her return to England, now aged seventy, with her husband, in a high state of prosperity and repentance.

NOTES AND GLOSSARY:

Gravesend: they are now quite along way down the Thames from London

the Downs: off Kent

the river came down from Limerick: Defoe refers to the River Shannon

freighter: (here) the man who organised the cargo on the ship

a charwoman: a woman who does domestic cleaning

this made me secure: this made me feel safe

it was not a story would bear telling: . . . *which* would bear . . .

night-fliers: Defoe explains this term in the ensuing sentence

land . . . cured: Moll and her fellows in the colonies have to prepare virgin land for cultivation

to look after: to look for

Spanish pistoles: valuable gold coins

Providence: God

a meeting-house: probably a prayer-house or chapel of a dissenting sect

scrivener: a kind of lawyer

fowling-pieces: guns

linen: underclothes and shirts

stuffs, serges: cloths

written in the year 1683: of course, Defoe wrote the novel in 1722. He had a tendency to set his stories well before the time of writing; his *Journal of the Plague Year*, for instance, also written in 1722, narrates the events of 1664–5

Part 3

Commentary

Moll's isolation

Defoe was interested in isolation, as must be apparent from the story of Robinson Crusoe. Moll Flanders, of course, far from living on a desert island, lives in the middle of a densely-peopled world, often in London itself; yet Defoe is at great pains to isolate her, too. She is always being abandoned. In the first forty-eight years of her life she is abandoned by, or has to abandon:

> her mother (who is transported);
> the gipsies (she escapes);
> the 'old woman' of Colchester (who dies);
> the 'elder brother' (who won't marry her);
> the 'younger brother' (Robin, who dies);
> her 'draper' husband (who has to flee abroad from his creditors);
> her third husband (who has to be left behind in Virginia because he turns out to be her brother);
> the Bath gentleman who is her lover (after a six-year liaison he repents his sinful life when he nearly dies of pleurisy);
> the banker who woos her (he can't get a divorce);
> her 'Lancashire husband' (they are too poor; he returns for a month but then abandons her *again*);
> the banker in London (who dies); and so on.

Moll is not always left penniless, but she is usually left alone and friendless and with penury imminent. She has few friends and no relations and often has to start a new life in a new place to disguise something in her past. This is as much as to say that she is new-born several times, in the almost total isolation created by taking on a new character.

At several points, in order to enable the plot to progress, Defoe has to create instantaneous new friends for Moll. As he keeps cutting her off relentlessly from any relatives, husbands, or long-term acquaintances, he has to introduce well-disposed but casual people to help her at awkward moments. Thus for instance, towards the end of the novel when Moll is setting herself up in America again, she meets a 'very honest Quaker' who tells her a good place to establish herself; this 'honest Quaker' is 'very helpful' and actually takes Moll to the place himself (Everyman p.285). If it were not for people such as this we would have to consider Moll a miracle of wisdom and luck, able to do everything for herself. As it is she is shown as being pretty resourceful and she is generally in charge in situations, even when there are men present.

Life as a market

Defoe is a tradesman and an economist. Everything in his world has a value, human beings included. Thus Moll is forever adding up how much she is worth and at almost any stage in the novel the reader, if he has been paying attention, can say how much money she possesses. Defoe is perhaps the first author in literature to concentrate more strongly on the realities of daily finance than on supposedly higher motives. It is this perhaps that earns him the title of the first real novelist; the implication is that the fiction that preceded *Robinson Crusoe* and *Moll Flanders* was largely romantic and unrealistic. Thus in *Moll Flanders*, Moll can only rarely afford to indulge in any higher motives than those of expediency; most of the time she operates on the level of market forces.

Moll is aware of this and comments on it frequently. 'I kept true to this notion,' she says (Everyman p.52) 'that a woman should never be kept for a mistress that had money to make herself a wife'. The men in her life are usually seen in the light of economic necessities rather than as romantic lovers, even when she actually likes them, as she often does, confessing at one point:

> he was the best-humoured merry sort of fellow that ever I met with; and I often reflected how doubly criminal it was to deceive such a man; but that necessity, which pressed me to a settlement suitable to my condition, was my authority for it.
>
> (Everyman p.68)

She is clearly very much enamoured of her Bath lover, who at first lives with her chastely. When they become lovers, she finds a strong 'inclination' towards him, but even here she comments on the economic significance of their transaction in unashamed terms:

> It is true that from the first hour I began to converse with him, I resolved to let him lie with me, if he offered it; but it was because I wanted his help, and knew of no other way of securing him . . . I was not without secret reproaches of my own conscience for the life I led . . . yet I had the terrible prospect of poverty and starving . . . as poverty brought me into it, so fear of poverty kept me in it.
>
> (Everyman p.102)

Poverty, necessity, distress, lack of a husband, lack of protection: these are the springs of vice in Defoe. His novel is studded with reminders of this fact (then less widely acknowledged than it is in our own day) and the overwhelming impression given is of life as a market:

> When a woman is thus left desolate and void of counsel, she is just like a bag of money or a jewel dropt on the highway, which is a prey to the next comer. (Everyman p.109)

So says Defoe, and one of Moll's husbands, when complaining of the wife he wishes to divorce so that he can marry Moll, complains that 'she is a whore not by necessity . . . but by inclination, and for the sake of the vice' (Everyman p.116). Later Moll suggests that people should offer up the prayer 'Give me not poverty, lest I steal' (Everyman p.163) which she says are the words of the wise man.

Moll, when young, can use her looks as a commodity which she sells in exchange for security, a husband, protection, food and drink. Later in life, impoverished and no longer marketable herself, she must turn to theft; she never really wants to sell herself or to steal, although Defoe, with one of his most disarming gestures, sometimes admits that she enjoys the things she basically regrets doing.

At the centre of the market-place of eighteenth-century life stood marriage. In an age when the only employment open to women was menial domestic work, a husband was the only alternative to prostitution or crime for those not prepared to be servants. A husband was an almost certain protection against poverty and want, and it was essential for a girl to get a husband at all costs. The literature of the eighteenth and nineteenth centuries, from Samuel Richardson (1689–1761) to Jane Austen (1775–1817) to George Eliot (1819–1880), is full of examples of the importance of marriage as an economic fact, but nobody perhaps is as explicit as Defoe about the market forces behind the marriage contract. In other writers these forces can be concealed behind other interesting themes: in Richardson's *Pamela* (1740) the interest centres on whether the poor girl will give in to the great squire and become his mistress or whether she will hold out and force him into marriage; in Fielding's *Tom Jones* (1749) the interest is in whether the young couple will be able to overcome the girl's father's opposition; and so on. But the market forces are always there (the real problem in *Pamela* is her poverty and low status; the only objection to Tom Jones marrying Sophia is that he is penniless); Defoe merely talks about them more openly than most. Marriage was a permanent institution involving the transfer and inheritance of property and was perhaps the major *economic* act in most people's lives, to be compared in that respect only with their dying. This was particularly true of the aristocracy and the rich, but it applied to the merchant and middle classes, too. Among the poorer classes marriage may have meant less in terms of the transfer of property, but it was still highly important for the lower-class girl to find someone to look after her in life.

Defoe, of course, deals with the middle classes, and in *Moll Flanders* we feel acutely the sense of insecurity of the bourgeois when poverty threatens. Moll herself learns early enough that, although it may be unromantic, marriage is generally regarded in an economic light, with love playing small part:

> This knowledge I soon learned by experience, viz., that the state of things was altered as to matrimony, that marriages were here the consequences of politic schemes, for forming interests, carrying on business, and that love had no share, or but very little, in the matter.
>
> (Everyman p.57)

Defoe is even able to put an economist's assessment of the marriage market into Moll's mouth:

> as the market ran all on the men's side, I found the women had lost the privilege of saying no . . . The men had such choice everywhere, that the case of the women was very unhappy; for they seemed to ply at every door, and if the man was by great chance refused at one house, he was sure to be received at the next.
>
> (Everyman p.58)

Here the mercantile imagery is obvious enough—Defoe envisages the men as customers, or dealers, who know that the market is on their side. So much is the matter weighted in favour of the men that they can even behave high-handedly towards women who have money: Defoe goes on to tell of one who nearly lost her man (by inquiring into his background) 'though she had near £2000 to her fortune'. Moll is always trying to get money, or to pretend that she has money, in order to attract men, and this even before her beauty has faded.

A good deal of the discussion in *Moll Flanders* between Moll and the reader consists of good advice, and much of this is connected with the marriage market; for instance:

> As for women that do not think their own safety worth their own thought, that, impatient of their present state, run into matrimony as a horse rushes into the battle, I can say nothing to them but this, that . . . they look like people that venture their estates in a lottery where there is a hundred thousand blanks to one prize.
>
> (Everyman p.64)

Here we hear the voice of the careful tradesman who warns against gambling and other methods of throwing one's money away. We hear it again in Moll's reflections on being a mistress: she saves money rather than spending it while she is being kept, knowing well enough that such things as these do not always continue; that men that keep mistresses often change them . . . and sometimes the ladies that are thus well used, are not careful by a prudent conduct to preserve the esteem of their persons, or the nice article of their fidelity, and then they are justly cast off with contempt.

(Everyman p.101)

Here Defoe's mercantile spirit is so concerned about the proper and prudent way of managing as a mistress that he quite ignores the possible immorality and degradation of the relationship itself, and reserves his scorn instead for mistresses who are not *'careful'* enough to play the game cleverly: these are *'justly'* cast off by their men. The word 'justly' here deserves some examination.

Moll's marriages are so closely bound up with her finances that it comes as no surprise to her (and not much to us) when she quotes one of her husbands as saying that 'he did not care to venture me too much upon the sea'. A wife worth something in goods, land, or money was a valuable property, not to be 'ventured'—'venture' in the seventeenth and eighteenth centuries being a word entirely associated with trade, investment and finance. Money would make a girl into a wife—lack of it would make her into a whore: it is almost as if the moral world is turned upside down, and for Moll it seems better to cheat and lie your way into the haven of matrimony than to risk the greater insecurity and immorality of prostitution; but she will turn even to that where necessity drives.

✳ Moll's morality ✳

In the great market-place of life it is hard for people to remain moral, as we have just seen. But Defoe, for all his respect for hard cash and hard facts, lived in a period when literature was expected to deal with moral issues from a largely Christian point of view, and he was not able or willing to ignore this expectation. He was, anyway, a Dissenter with a Puritan background, and preaching has always come naturally to such people. As a result *Moll Flanders* is full of moral commentary, and we find Defoe frequently looking over his shoulder, as it were, to make sure that his rather immoral tale can be seen as a warning or an example that will benefit the reader. The whole of the Author's Preface can be read in this light: Defoe is obviously on the horns of a dilemma here, between his instinct as an artist to create the most attractive possible work, and his tendency as a Puritan to regard fiction as being merely a vehicle for morality.

In the Preface he claims first that Moll's story is true; then he is able to say that 'All possible care . . . has been taken to give no lewd ideas, no immodest turns in the new dressing up of this story' (Everyman p.1). Next, he congratulates himself on having omitted some of the worst parts of Moll's life, and then he justifies the bad parts he has included:

> To give the history of a wicked life repented of, necessarily requires that the wicked part should be made as wicked as the real history of it will bear, to illustrate and give a beauty to the penitent part, which is certainly the best and brightest . . .   (Everyman p.2)

In all this we can feel Defoe twisting uncomfortably between the claims of his art and those of his dissenting conscience. He cannot admit that *Moll Flanders* is an invented tale; if he does he can be condemned for inventing so much immorality: he pretends that he has only put in enough of the immorality to set off the 'penitent part' which he claims to prefer. And yet the life and vigour of the novel are surely to be found in Moll's energetic and often 'immoral' self-defence, by whatever means, against the world, and Defoe the artist knows that it is through this that he will catch the reader's attention. What is more, the 'penitent part' is not exactly a repudiation of the immoral part. When we come to the end of the novel we are inclined to feel that Moll's repentance is no contradiction of her previous life but a confirmation of it: now she has saved her body she can afford to save her soul; the most profitable thing to do, for an old woman who no longer needs to struggle for her bread, is to invest in heaven.

Later in the Preface, Defoe turns to another sort of justification for the immoralities in his novel and maintains that by reading about street robberies and Moll's other tricks and thefts we will be warned against people like her. The cautious tradesman here advises his fellow tradesmen how to avoid being robbed.

These attitudes which Defoe displays in the Preface form the basis of Moll's own morality in the novel. She, too, takes a certain delight in her life of crime, but knows all along that she had better be careful and repent in the end. She, too, offers her tale as a warning to others. But outweighing these notions are the all-pervading demands of necessity (as discussed in the last section) and a good deal of simple commonsense, both of which lead Moll far from strict Christian morality.

Thus, for instance, when Moll parts from her Bath lover, because he has repented of their sinful affair, she needs to get as much money out of him as possible in order to survive, and she invents the tale that she is going to cross over to America:

> This was indeed all a cheat thus far, viz., that I had no intention to go to Virginia, as the account of my former affairs there may convince anybody of; but the business was to get this last £50 of him, if possible, knowing well enough it would be the last penny I was ever to expect.
> (Everyman p.107)

We are hardly likely to condemn Moll, driven as she is by the prospect of poverty, for squeezing a little more money out of a rich man who, after all, is abandoning her. And yet, like Defoe, she has a conscience in the midst of her immoralities:

> Then it occurred to me, 'What an abominable creature am I! and how is this innocent gentleman going to be abused by me!'
> (Everyman p.156)

Nonetheless she goes ahead and marries her 'innocent gentleman' without telling him of her life of thieving, incest and whoredom. What else can she do?

Moll's moralising seems to echo the standard Puritan warnings with the addition of Defoe's own commercial instincts. She is given the language of the sermon at times:

> how much happier a life of virtue and sobriety is, than that which we call a life of pleasure!　(Everyman p.161)

> As covetousness is the root of all evil, so poverty is the worst of all snares.　(Everyman p.161)

This, however, tends to include an element of Puritan prudentialism, and Defoe the merchant lends a special meaning to these moral sentiments. Thus when Moll reflects on her gradual descent into a life of crime she employs the standard preacher's description of her sinfulness creeping up on her little by little:

> 'yet the resolution I had formerly taken of leaving off this horrid trade when I had gotten a little more, did not return, but I must get still more . . .'

So far this is entirely Christian, but then Defoe adds,

> and the avarice had such success, that I had no more thoughts of coming to a timely alteration of life, though without it I could expect no safety, no tranquility in the possession of what I had gained . . .
> (Everyman p.178)

Defoe seems almost not to have noticed that he has slipped out of Christian preaching here and is allowing Moll to regret that she did not leave off stealing *when she had made enough to live comfortably on what she had 'gained'*. The voice of the prudent tradesman here overcomes the voice of the moralist.

Later we find an even more striking example of the two voices:

> I was now in good circumstances indeed, if I could have known my time for leaving off . . . I had £700 by me in money, besides clothes, rings, some plate and two gold watches, and all of them stolen . . . Oh! had I even now had the grace of repentance . . . (Everyman p.218)

Moll wants, literally, to have the best of both worlds: she wants her stolen wealth, safety to enjoy it, and time to repent so that she will be saved.

Necessity drives Moll to be immoral, she wants to repent and she expresses Christian horror at her own immorality; but the main feeling left in the reader's mind is that as sin is the product of poverty, the best thing is to get rich and then avoid sin. Above all a life of sin is insecure: guilt makes Moll unhappy ('I had a weight of guilt upon me, enough to sink any creature who had the least power of reflection left' Everyman p.240) and her life of crime is dangerous and uncertain—both in this world, where it leads to the gallows, and in the life to come, where it leads to hell. Everything therefore points to getting rich and then leading a secure, moral, guilt-free life. Moll only reaches this heaven at the very end of her story.

Defoe's imagery

At the end of the last section a comparison was made between this life and the next: Moll is trying to secure herself both in this world and in heaven. Defoe takes this point up and develops a picture of how the life of insecurity leads to hell, the result of crime (sin) in particular being prison (hell). This naturally appears at the point of Moll's first committal to Newgate, 'that horrid place!' Moll's description of her first impressions of this infamous prison could apply to hell:

> 'tis impossible to describe the terror of my mind, when I was first brought in, and when I looked around upon all the horrors of that dismal place. I looked on myself as lost . . . the hellish noise, the roaring, swearing and clamour, the stench and nastiness, and all the dreadful afflicting things that I saw there, joined to make the place seem an emblem of hell itself, and a kind of entrance into it.
>
> (Everyman p.236)

A few paragraphs later Moll asks one of her fellow-prisoners how she felt when she first arrived in Newgate and discovers 'that she thought she was in hell'. (Everyman p.237)

All this, of course, is a piece of extended imagery which I have dealt with at some length because it demonstrates that Defoe is *not* a writer who relies on this device. In the example it will be seen that he is not willing simply to leave the reader to make the obvious equation Newgate = hell. Instead he introduces the word 'hellish' to describe the noise there, then specifically likens it to hell, even calling it an 'emblem' (image) of that place, and then a few paragraphs later he reverts to the notion again. It is as if here, early in the history of the novel, the subtle use of imagery that is so common among the masters of the genre has not yet developed. One result of this is that Defoe tends to use similes rather than metaphors, similes being simpler and more obvious images. Thus, in describing the effect of Moll's association with criminals on her, he says,

> like the water in the hollows of mountains, which petrifies and turns into stone whatever they are suffered to drop upon; so the continual conversing with such a crew of hell-hounds had the same common operation upon me as upon other people.　　　(Everyman p.240)

Here the main image is an imaginative one, laid out formally like an epic simile in Homer or Virgil. The second part of the sentence, if examined closely, reveals some buried imagery which needs explanation. The first point, however, is that Defoe uses large-scale imagery very rarely, rather obviously, and for preference in the form of a simile. Grand symbolism and extended metaphor are not in his style; he is an open and straightforward writer, concerned with facts and common reality rather than with flights of imagination or mysticism.

His 'buried' images do not really contradict this. In the example given above he calls Moll's fellow-criminals 'a crew of hell-hounds' and here there are two images: first a 'crew' instead of a 'group' or 'band', and 'hell-hounds' instead of 'criminals'. These words come naturally to Defoe as part of the slang of his day and are surely not conscious imagery as such. 'Crew' in fact, still meant a 'group' or 'band' in a non-metaphorical sense in 1722, which indicates the care needed when dealing with eighteenth-century English; while 'hell-hound' was firmly established in the language in its Middle English phase (AD 1100–1500) to mean any depraved person. These buried images may not have any more force as images than the word 'bonnet' when used today to refer to the part of a car which conceals the engine.

Generally, then, Defoe uses little imagery, and what he does use is either very clearly done or so 'buried' as not really to count.

Defoe's narration

The whole of *Moll Flanders* is narrated by Moll in the first person. Only the Preface gives us an objective view of her: Defoe does not employ the device of having other characters talking or writing about Moll (in conversations or letters) to any extent, so we are constantly watching her and her actions through her own eyes. This has a number of benefits for Defoe, and one or two disadvantages.

The first benefit he derives is immediacy. We feel as though we are in the thick of the action with Moll. She sounds as though she is talking to us directly and we catch her tones of excitement, horror and anxiety straight from her own mouth, as it were.

②   The second benefit Defoe derives from Moll's first-person narration is what we might call 'false authenticity'. We know that Defoe, anxious about the status of fiction, dressed up his novels as true stories; naturally, Moll's story somehow seems truer, although it is not, because we have the illusion that she is telling it herself.

③   The third benefit is authenticity. Defoe is able to perform his task as a novelist (particularly from the point of view of looking into what is *really* happening behind the surface actions) far more easily because he can appeal directly to Moll's consciousness of herself. Through her he can immediately give a guaranteed authentic picture of what his heroine thinks or feels at any given stage.

Of these three benefits it is the first which gives Defoe his characteristic voice and is the main feature of his style. Hiding behind the persona of Moll, he does not need to be too concerned about writing beautiful English, about the balance and structure of sentences and paragraphs, or about the lack of outside references in his prose. Take, for instance, a short paragraph such as this (Moll is referring to a visit of the good minister to her in prison):

> This discourse left a kind of sadness on my heart, as if I might expect the affair would have a tragical issue still, which, however, he had no certainty of; yet I did not at that time question him about it, he having said he would do his utmost to bring it to a good end, and that he hoped he might, but he would not have me be secure; and the consequence showed that he had reason for what he said.
>
> (Everyman p.252)

This cannot be described as beautiful or elegant English prose; it has no interesting vocabulary, no figures of speech, above all no balance or symmetry, nor does it pause at all to refer to anything outside itself; it is not witty or moving. But it does sound extremely like a woman recounting a visit and telling us what her visitor said. First her emotion is identified (sadness) and an explanation is immediately given for it; then the minister's uncertainty is mentioned and at once the reader feels the question springing up, 'Well, didn't you *ask* him what was going to happen? If not, why not?' So Moll answers the reader at once and trails off with some quotations from the minister's earlier visit, reminding us as she reminds herself that it is better to trust a good man than to nag him. Finally she observes that the minister was proved right about not being too cautious, so we are agog to discover what comes next.

There is a considerable economy in this direct and immediate narration: Defoe saves pages of possibly tedious dialogue and we are at once masters of the situation.

The disadvantages of Defoe's style have been mentioned or hinted at in the last section and in what has been said in this. He is debarred from a number of literary possibilities that might help him: he cannot employ extensive or subtle imagery; he cannot transcend the limits of Moll's mind; above all, he cannot refer to some apt quotation or story or generalisation that comes from outside the world of the novel. As a result his novel seems rather flat and mundane, and cut off from the mainstream of eighteenth-century cultural life. *Moll Flanders* seems strangely alien beside the works of Swift, Pope and Fielding. Moll herself is unable to get a perspective on society as a whole, and Defoe is prevented from achieving a coherent moral attitude; it is in the end perhaps true to say that *Moll Flanders* is an interesting novel in detail but that its overall purpose and significance remain unclear.

Defoe's world: the law, cruelty, money and society

Defoe is a realist, which means that his fiction aims to convey a credible impression of daily life. Not surprisingly, then, this picture has to be based very closely on the realities of the world in which he lived. This world of 1722, very different from our own, should be carefully thought about by the student of *Moll Flanders*.

First of all it is worth remembering that in the Britain of Defoe's day the laws against stealing were at their harshest stage. The law had never been soft on thieves, but the number of offences for which death was the punishment rose in the seventeenth century and continued to rise during the eighteenth, when the notorious Game Laws and others multiplied the severity of punishments and the trivial nature of the offences for which they were handed out. It has been estimated that during most of the eighteenth century there were some two hundred crimes for which hanging was the appropriate punishment as well as a number of crimes (such as the 'coining' Moll refuses to undertake) for which the punishment was to be burnt at the stake. The principal reason for this brutal legislation was that society did not know what else to do with its criminals. The notion of rehabilitation through a period in prison belongs to the nineteenth century; in the eighteenth, society preferred simply to get rid of troublesome elements, and death is obviously the quickest way to achieve this.

Another advantage of widespread capital punishment seemed to be that it could deter people from becoming criminals (although it does not seem to have been very effective in this, as *Moll Flanders* testifies). Executions were therefore public and to some extent stage-managed to create the maximum effect. As we discover in the prison episodes of *Moll Flanders*, a 'dead warrant' was produced weekly in Newgate, with perhaps half-a-dozen names on it of people who were to die; these were chosen from among the people already condemned to death but kept in prison until a suitable moment. On execution day certain church bells would toll mournfully, the condemned would be taken in procession on the back of a cart to Tyburn (now Marble Arch) and hanged, dying slowly by strangulation, not quickly by having their necks broken. The public would crowd around and seats in specially erected stands would sell for high prices.

Not all judges and juries were happy to see so many people hang, however, and it was fortunate that the colonisation of America was proceeding rapidly during the eighteenth century, because large numbers of criminals were got rid of by being 'transported' (as Moll is) to the New World. This was an equally good way of removing unwanted elements from society; a provision was always made that the transported convict should not return to Britain in less than a stated number of years. It is apparent from Moll's story that personal influence and money could go some way towards avoiding both the gallows and the discomforts of transportation.

It was a heartless and cruel world by our standards, at least for such as Moll who could not afford to be sentimental. This is particularly apparent when Moll is among criminals, but it appears elsewhere, too. When she is preparing to have a baby, for instance, the midwife who is quoting her various prices for the lying-in, says quite naturally,

'Then madam . . . if the child should not live, as it sometimes happens, there is the minister's article saved . . .'

Moll comments on this and one or two other proposed economies by saying,

'This was the most reasonable thing that I ever heard of; so I smiled . . .'
(Everyman p.141)

It is hard to imagine a modern pregnant woman smiling so easily in a discussion of the death of her baby, but of course infant mortality is now uncommon, while in Defoe's day it was at least 50 per cent in most years.

This more cruel world is, of course, the natural background to the novel, and it is worth thinking about the reality that lies behind such things as Defoe's passing references to bear-baiting and people being beaten to death in the street, to duels and the press-gang. When we consider the high elegance of Georgian architecture and clothing and the polish and wit of the poetry of Pope, we must always remember this darker side of eighteenth-century life, particularly in London.

Another aspect of Defoe's world that is worth noticing concerns the value of money. We are lucky that the tradesman in Defoe gave him a fascination with costs and figures, because *Moll Flanders* thus becomes a sort of encyclopaedia of the cost of living at that time. The principal result of an investigation into Defoe's figures is that an enormous gap opens up between the basic cost of daily survival—which seems extremely cheap—and the cost of anything luxurious or gentlemanly—which seems extremely expensive. Thus, when Moll is in Lancashire being courted by her penniless Irish suitor, he spends 'three or four' *hundred* pounds on the hire of coaches and servants to impress her, over a period of a few months at most; when they are married and reveal their mutual poverty, Moll offers him thirty-one pounds saying, 'I expected it would maintain me three or four years' (Everyman p.127). This, in effect, amounts to the proposition that a man, to look like a gentleman, could spend *ten times* as much in a few months as a single woman would need to 'maintain' herself for several years. To bring Moll's thirty-one pounds up to modern values (1980) we would have to multiply it by some two or three hundred times, which means that if we do the same for her suitor's coaches and servants and clothes, he spent at least sixty thousand pounds, in modern values, on a few months' courting.

These calculations are extremely revealing. We live in a world where most people fall within quite a narrow income-band, but in Defoe's world the gap between rich and poor was immense; and with no pensions, trade unions, or social security, it was an insecure world in which lack of money was not only immediately obvious but devastating in its effect. To be a gentleman required a considerable fortune, which could only be acquired by inheritance or marriage; to be without the expensive outward signs of gentility was to be debarred from civilised society and, indeed, could mean being left to starve. The astonishing thing is how Moll, although an orphan, a servant, a prostitute and a thief, is consistent in her desire to be 'a gentlewoman'. She has to make do with some middle-class husbands and lovers, but she is happiest either at the bottom end of society, where her sums of money can keep her going for a long time, or at the top, riding about in a coach with a fine gentleman beside her.

The picture of society which these points give us is one of radical isolation: the law wants only to isolate and eradicate the erring individual, to send him abroad or to his grave; the cruelty of the time indicates a lack of human warmth and sympathy; the financial precariousness of life is such that each man has to look out for himself, either stealing in anonymity or trying to get married under a false identity. *Moll Flanders*, like *Robinson Crusoe*, is an epic of this isolation.

On the other hand, Defoe is not entirely inhuman. He sees the individual as a being left often enough to his or her own resources, but he is aware of the importance of society in an almost contradictory way. He puts into Moll's mouth the following speech about children:

It is manifest to all that understand anything of children, that we are born into the world helpless, and uncapable either to supply our own wants or so much as make them known; and that without help we must perish; and this help requires not only an assisting hand, whether of the mother or somebody else, but there are two things necessary in that assisting hand, that is, care and skill . . .

(Everyman p.148)

Strangely enough, in writing *Moll Flanders* Defoe is attempting a novel about a woman who, from the earliest possible moment, had to dispense with the care and skill of assisting hands and fend for herself. Defoe preferred not to take his thesis about children a step further and emphasise the interdependence of adults. As a result *Moll Flanders* is quite unlike the great novels of the nineteenth century which often give a broad and deep impression of an interdependent society. In George Eliot's *Middlemarch* (1871–2), for instance, or even in *Vanity Fair* (1847–8) by William Thackeray (whose heroine is a criminal at times and could be compared interestingly with Moll) we have a sense of the total structure of social life. Defoe's novel may seem a little thin in comparison with these.

Part 4

Hints for study

Points for detailed study

Moll's character

This is the heart of the book. She narrates the entire novel and every-thing is presented as it happens to her or as it affects her. A question that arises here is whether she is altered by her experiences or whether she alters her environment because of being who she is. The best answer to this might be that she remains much the same throughout the novel, but that different circumstances bring out different aspects of her character. Thus:

Moll is clever. This cleverness emerges honourably enough when she is a child but it is put to criminal use when she becomes a thief. It enables her to avoid arrest for a remarkably long time.

Moll is calculating. She knows how to charm people and if they are nice people the charm is genuine, but if they threaten her she immediately starts to conceal things beneath the charm of the surface. For instance, she charms her Lancashire husband and even manages to behave decently towards him when he reveals he is penniless. As soon as she discovers this, however, she at once conceals half her money from him while appearing openly to offer him all she has. (Everyman p.12/ff.)

Moll is unfeeling except where she can afford to be. She disposes of children and husbands without many words of regret when it is most convenient to do so. But when, as for example at the end of the novel, a child is useful to her and she can afford to stay near him, she shows signs of genuine gratitude and affection.

It would also be worth looking at the points in the novel where Moll is faced with choices: should she marry Robin (the 'younger brother'), should she take to crime and prostitution? Usually she has no option, but sometimes she hints at the bent of her own character towards a certain course of action.

Defoe's defensiveness

Moll says at one point, 'I am giving an account of what was, not of what ought or ought not to be' (Everyman p.84). This is the central point in Defoe's defence against his critics. By saying that Moll's story is *true* he refutes simultaneously the charges (*a*) that his work is fictional and (*b*) that he has included an excessive amount of immorality. It is worth examining *Moll Flanders* for other examples of this defensiveness, which may be accounted for by the fact that serious fiction was not a properly established genre in 1722, as well as by Defoe's Puritan consciousness.

Sometimes this defensiveness leads Defoe to moralise in a way that stands out from the mainstream of his story in a rather uncomfortable way, as if he had just remembered that he must condemn the wickednesses he delights in narrating. Thus he has Moll comment on an excellent and discreet midwife:

> Let none be encouraged in their loose practices from this dexterous lady's management, for she has gone to her place [hell?], and I dare say has left nothing behind her that can or will come up to it.
>
> (Everyman p.146)

The moralising here is clearly only an aside, an afterthought. It starts in the sententious tones of the preacher and indicates that this wicked woman has gone to hell, but it concludes by pointing out that the real reason for not relying on discreet midwives for giving birth to illegitimate children is that girls would be unlikely to find such a good one.

On the other hand, Defoe can sometimes admit frankly that he is not primarily interested in the moral aspects of Moll's tale. When her last husband becomes penitent (when he discovers how rich he is going to be in America—not before) and Moll has described his new goodness she concludes this part of her story with the open admission to her readers that,

> I could fill a larger history than this with the evidences of this truth [her husband's reformed character], but that I doubt that part of the story will not be equally diverting as the wicked part.
>
> (Everyman p.292)

It should be added, finally, that Defoe is also capable of including moral notions in his story without making them seem like alien bodies. When Moll traps, seduces and robs a drunken gentleman, for instance, she remarks,

> There is nothing so absurd, so surfeiting, so ridiculous, as a man heated by wine in his head, and a wicked gust in his inclination together . . .
>
> (Everyman p.194)

This whole passage is worth studying for its very natural and integrated moralising.

Defoe's sentences

Defoe writes an English style that is different from almost anyone else's. (See sections on Defoe's imagery and narration, pp.42–5.) It is a good idea for the student of *Moll Flanders* to examine his prose to see why this is. It seems that it is principally a matter of his sentence-length and the balance of the clauses (or lack of balance) in them. Paragraphs are important, too, and the brisk exchanges of his passages of dialogue. But the basic Defoe sentence is nearly always recognisable. Why?

The structure of Moll's story

Does *Moll Flanders* have a structure? Obviously it has the basic one of Moll's life, stretching as it does over the seventy years of a normal human existence. But is there anything in the way of development, climax or resolution? The full title of the novel is *The Fortunes and Misfortunes of the famous Moll Flanders*; and the novel is just that, a series of happy and unhappy episodes in a long life. We could compare it in this respect with novels like *David Copperfield* (1849–50) by Charles Dickens (1812–70) from the nineteenth century, or *Sons and Lovers* (1913) by D.H. Lawrence (1885–1930) or *Portrait of the Artist as a Young Man* (1914–15) by James Joyce (1882–1941), from the twentieth century. In all these novels the hero is seen developing (the technical name for this sort of novel is *Bildungsroman*), although this is more marked in Lawrence and Joyce than in Dickens, and their structure depends respectively on the increasing awareness and moral perception of their heroes, of David, of Paul Morel, and of Stephen Dedalus. This is not true of Moll. She is very much the same at the end of the novel as she is at the beginning. We want her to avoid the gallows and settle down happily and at last she does this, but the route she travels towards this ending is not interesting as a pattern of development, only as a series of colourful and cautionary episodes. In this way *Moll Flanders* is a true picaresque narrative (see Introduction, p.6) and perhaps operates more on the surface level (immediate social questions, adventures, action, morals) than on the deeper levels the novel was later to achieve (psychological depths, broad social issues, personal development).

Selection of quotations

Moll Flanders is an easy novel from which to quote, and essays about it should be full of quotation. Remember that in nearly every case it is Moll herself who is speaking, not Defoe, although it is clear that Defoe's voice sometimes comes through and, of course, as author he is responsible for all that Moll says. Students could look at the use made of quotations in the Introduction and Commentary in these Notes to get an immediate idea of how it can be done. Quotation *by itself* is, of course, almost useless: passages from the original text should be *introduced* and then if necessary *commented on*.

In most cases it is a good idea to quote from several different places in the novel to establish a point. Thus for instance, if you want to make clear that Moll is an extremely *secretive* and *prudent* woman, it may not be enough simply to quote once; after all, she has a great number of adventures and one example of prudence could be an aberration, but the following examples put together should convince the reader:

Moll is always careful not to give too much away and it is typical of her to remark 'I told him so much of my story as I thought convenient . . .'.

(see Everyman p.257)

Even when Moll is among friends she keeps important information to herself, for instance not telling her old 'governess', who has been most loyal to her, that the man she is crossing to America with is her husband.

(see Everyman p.265)

Above all, Moll is prudent about money, never telling anyone the full extent of her fortune at a given moment. Even when she is on board the ship that will take her and her final husband to America and he tells her truly how much money he has, she says: 'I gave him an account of my stock as faithfully that is to say, what I had taken with me; for I was resolved, whatever should happen, to keep what I had left in reserve . . .'

(Everyman p.269)

Moll cannot be open even at this point—life has taught her the merits of prudence.

Thus, although Moll's story rushes forward and does not refer back to itself or create a moral pattern, it does contain repetitions of similar actions on her part and it is these that should be accumulated for quotation and question-answering.

Answering questions on *Moll Flanders*

First, do not neglect the history of the time: try to include some references to the historical background of the novel. Show that you do not think of it as existing in a vacuum. This does not necessarily mean that you should quote streams of dates, but that you should demonstrate some notion of what early eighteenth-century life might have been like for a woman, a criminal, a prisoner and so on. There are some useful and entertaining books on the period in general (see Suggestions for further reading, page 58).

Second, do not neglect the history of the novel. Show that you are aware of the difference it makes that *Moll Flanders* was written in 1722, before Richardson and before Fielding. Especially for the Puritan Defoe, the current idea of fiction as light entertainment, unrealistic and unserious, meant that he had to present his story in a certain way. Some of the more sophisticated methods of later novelists were unavailable to him. On the other hand, this point must not be exaggerated: *Don Quixote*, by the Spanish writer Miguel de Cervantes (1547–1616), a very great novel indeed, appeared between 1605 and 1615, being translated into English (first part) in 1612; furthermore, some of the devices of fiction were available to earlier writers of verse: Homer uses flashbacks and patterns of imagery in a way that is never found in Defoe's work.

Your basic material for answering questions, however, must come from the text itself. This means that constant quotation and reference are necessary and that you should try to impress your reader with a sense of your intimate knowledge of the detail of the novel. Try to keep the narration uppermost in your mind, thinking about Moll and the way she is telling her story. Remember that Defoe, a non-criminal man, is here purporting to enter into the thoughts of a criminal woman. How far does he succeed in this? Is his text marred by there being a gap between him and Moll?

Specimen questions on *Moll Flanders*

1. *Discuss Moll's role as narrator of* Moll Flanders.

In *Moll Flanders*, Moll has to act as the mouthpiece for Defoe and as the narrator of her own remarkable story. As a result she has two different voices which to some extent contradict one another, as she sometimes speaks as the prudent and cautionary Mr Defoe, and sometimes as the racy and reckless Moll.

The novel opens with the narrative firmly in Moll's own hands. 'My name is so well known in the records or registers at Newgate', she says (Everyman p.7) and at once we feel that we are being taken into her confidence. The first page is full of the word 'I' and later pages do not differ from this. Here is a woman talking of herself; she is not an omniscient narrator as is demonstrated by the fact that she cannot talk about any period of her life earlier than her first memories. She is very much a first-person narrator limited to first-hand experiences. When Defoe wants her to talk of things outside her immediate knowledge he is

careful to make her attribute her awareness of them to an informant;
for instance:

> I have been told, that in one of our neighbour nations, whether it be
> in France or where else I know not, they have an order from the king..
>
> (Everyman p.7)

and:

> The circumstances [of her mother's transportation] are too long to
> repeat, and I have heard them related so many ways, that I can scarce
> tell which is the right account.
>
> (Everyman p.8)

For most of the time, however, Moll talks out of her own memory, very
directly and vividly. The effect of this is to allow us to enter into her
emotions and reactions more intimately than we would be able to do if
Defoe told her story in the third person. Here is a typical example of
Moll's narrative:

> The circumstances I was in made the offer of a good husband the
> most necessary thing in the world to me, but I found soon that to be
> made cheap and easy was not the way.
>
> (Everyman p.65)

This sort of narration—direct and to the point—suits Moll's character,
which is frank and unafraid, and it easily lets the reader into the work-
ings of her mind. We can tell even in this short quotation (which seems
unremarkable enough) that Moll thinks about how she should present
herself to the world, that she for her own part would be prepared to be
'cheap and easy' but that it will not serve her turn, and so on.

These are all confessions. Moll is not ashamed of what she has done
and she is quite willing to tell all. We tend to forget the fact that she is
supposedly recounting her life story at the age of seventy, because she
throws herself into each new adventure with such verve and vigour that
it seems to be happening all over again before our very eyes. The astonishing description of her first impressions of Newgate, for instance
(Everyman p.236) come to us much as they first came to Moll. She does
not pause to impose much distance between her present self and her
past selves. For the greater part of the novel she rushes forward in a
breathless haste of first-person narration of the most immediate, naïve
and revealing sort.

However, there is another narrative voice in *Moll Flanders*. This is
the voice of Daniel Defoe. It is the voice (supposedly still Moll's of
course) which generalises, comments on the action, moralises, and
discusses the wider implications of the actions we witness. Character-
istically it is heard less often than Moll's own voice, and noticeably it is

disinclined to use the 'I' of first-person narration. Take the following sentence for example; it makes up one entire paragraph:

> No man of common sense will value a woman the less for not giving herself up at the first attack, or for not accepting his proposal without inquiring into his person or character; on the contrary, he must think her the weakest of all creatures, as the rate of men now goes; in short he must have a very contemptible opinion of her capacities, that having but one cast for her life, shall cast that life away at once, and make matrimony, like death, be a leap in the dark.
>
> (Everyman p.64)

Here it is notionally Moll speaking, but the voice is that of a man talking to fellow men, and it is the voice of a thoughtful moraliser on life and death. The word 'I' makes no appearance and instead we are treated to a pause in the action—a moment for general reflection, a moment for advice not dissimilar from the advice Defoe offers about street robberies and other interesting topics.

This 'objective' voice (which we can contrast with the 'subjective' voice in which Moll recounts her adventures) contradicts Moll's other voice at times. When, for instance, it stresses the helplessness of children, we cannot help remembering Moll's own capacity for looking after herself:

> . . . we are born into the world helpless, and uncapable either to supply our own wants or so much as make them known . . .
>
> (Everyman p.148)

This is a fair piece of conventional eighteenth-century moralising which seems to have little to do with Moll's own considerable determination to look after herself.

The gap between the two narrative voices in *Moll Flanders* may explain the novel's superficiality. We feel that the 'moral' Moll (the 'objective' voice; Defoe in fact) is abstract, general and cool while Moll 'herself' (the 'subjective' voice, 'I') is particular, concrete and warmly involved. As a result, when this interesting and adventurous woman pauses to give us the benefit of her wisdom, we find she at once loses the vigorous charm she possessed as the other kind of narrator.

---

2. *How does Defoe present Moll's reactions to the episodes and adventures of her life?*

(*i*) Moll lives in a hard world with few advantages; she is an orphan, without family, friends or money. The early eighteenth century was a hard time for unprotected women. Therefore she has to develop a tough shell to defend herself against the world. Give examples.

(*ii*) Defoe presents this process in Moll in her own words. She is look-ing back from the end of a long life; but she enters freshly into the narration of her old adventures. Give examples.

(*iii*) Generally speaking, Defoe has Moll *explain* why things happen to her, *narrate* how they happened, *comment* on the moral and other results of them, and finally *summarise* the position she is left in afterwards in terms of money, children, and so on.

(*iv*) All this is done with great immediacy: Moll quotes the words people use, describes actions and objects in detail, remembers her every emotion. This would be very unusual for a seventy-year-old woman in reality.

(*v*) Defoe needs Moll as a presenter to overcome the charge that what he is writing is mere fantasy.

---

3. *Is* Moll Flanders *concerned with the liberation of the female sex?*

(*i*) The position of women in the eighteenth century was not one of utter subjection, but their sphere of action was strictly limited, except perhaps in the criminal world. Quote historical text if possible.

(*ii*) This position of women is apparent from *Moll Flanders*. In certain spheres Moll can do well, particularly as a thief and, where neces-sary, as a mistress or a prostitute. However, she cannot operate entirely freely—she desperately needs someone, usually a man, to protect her. Even where she is stronger than the man she needs him.

(*iii*) Moll is thus not a 'liberated' woman. She recognises the masculine realities of her world and does not seem to object to them in principle.

(*iv*) There is a sense, however, underlying Moll's story, of absolute equality between men and women. If Moll never objects to the privileges of men, she equally never sees men as her superiors. If she accepts without question that she is debarred from certain spheres of activity (and women played no part in political or public life in Defoe's day, nor were they involved in any profession or any commerce above the simplest level) within the remaining spheres she is generally more clever and more determined than the man she is with. She saves her Lancashire husband by her quick thinking; she is the moving spirit behind their eventual rehabilitation in the New World; and, as a symbolic example, when she tries acting as a thief in men's clothes, she soon rejects them and obviously prefers her female attire.

(*v*) This equality (which may arise because Defoe, a man, is writing the story) is one of the strongest impressions left by the novel. In Richardson's *Pamela*, Fielding's *Tom Jones* and the other great eighteenth-century novels (as well as in Jane Austen, 1775–1817, and Dickens) we feel women to be a sex that must be seen as dependent, whose existence is somehow contingent upon that of men. *Moll Flanders* puts a woman in a position of strength and self-reliance that was unequalled in fiction until the twentieth century.

4. *Discuss Defoe's language*

(*i*) Defoe uses a large proportion of Anglo-Saxon-based words. In particular he does not use a great number of Latin- and Greek-based words. Give examples.

(*ii*) Writing as he did at a time of high neo-classicism, this is perhaps surprising. Here is an 'Augustan' who writes without apparently using the 'Augustan' language. Refer to his contemporaries.

(*iii*) But Defoe was not elaborately educated, did not attend university (Dissenters could not do so), and was writing for a more popular audience than Pope or Swift. He wanted to tell a good tale and make some money.

(*iv*) So *Moll Flanders* is written in colloquial and unstylish English. Moll speaks a good deal more realistically than many heroines, and Defoe's grammar, language and tone are all aimed at representing the natural flow of her thoughts. Give examples.

(*v*) Sometimes when he wishes to preach or theorise a little, Defoe's language rises to the occasion. Give examples.

Some other questions

(1) Discuss *Moll Flanders* as a novel of isolation.
(2) Compare Moll with some later heroines in fiction with which you are familiar.
(3) What use does Defoe make of the law in the machinery of his novel?
(4) Discuss the apparently structureless nature of Moll's narrative.

Part 5

Suggestions for further reading

The text

Moll Flanders, *ed.* David J. Johnson, Everyman's Library, Dent, London, 1972; and *ed.* Juliet Mitchell, Penguin English Library, Penguin Books, Harmondsworth, 1978.

Other works by Daniel Defoe

Robinson Crusoe; available in many editions, including Penguin and Everyman.

A Journal of the Plague Year, *ed.* Louis Landa, Oxford University Press, 1969; and *ed.* D.J. Johnson, Everyman's Library, Dent, London, 1966.

Captain Singleton, *ed.* Shiv. K. Kumar, Oxford Univerity Press, 1969; and *ed.* James Sutherland, Everyman's Library, Dent, London, 1963.

Roxana, *ed.* Jane Jack, Oxford University Press, 1964.

Colonel Jack, *ed.* S.H. Monk, Oxford University Press, 1965, paperback 1970.

Criticism and general reading

BYRD (ED.): *Defoe*, in Twentieth-Century Views, Prentice-Hall, New Jersey, 1976.

EARLE, PETER: *The World of Defoe*, Weidenfeld & Nicholson, London, 1976.

FREEMAN, WILLIAM: *The Incredible Defoe*, Herbert Jenkins, London, 1950.

MOORE, J.R.: *Daniel Defoe: Citizen of the Modern World*, Chicago University Press, 1958.

PLUMB, J.H.: England in the Eighteenth Century, Penguin Books, Harmondsworth, 1966.

ROGERS, PAT (ED.): *Defoe: The Critical Heritage*, Routledge & Kegan Paul, London, 1972.

SUTHERLAND, JAMES: *Defoe*, Methuen, London, 2nd edition 1950.

The author of these notes

LANCE ST JOHN BUTLER was educated at Pembroke College, Cambridge. He taught English in Iraq, Algeria and London before working for a year as a banker in Brazil. He was a lecturer in English at King Abdulaziz University, Jeddah, Saudi Arabia (1970–1), then a post-graduate student at the University of East Anglia (1971–2) before becoming a lecturer at the University of Stirling in 1972. He has edited *Thomas Hardy after Fifty Years* (1977) and written *Thomas Hardy* (1978). He is also the author of York Notes on Fielding's *Tom Jones* and Lawrence's *Sons and Lovers*.

York Notes: list of titles

CHINUA ACHEBE
A Man of the People
Arrow of God
Things Fall Apart

EDWARD ALBEE
Who's Afraid of Virginia Woolf?

ELECHI AMADI
The Concubine

ANONYMOUS
Beowulf
Everyman

AYI KWEI ARMAH
The Beautyful Ones Are Not Yet Born

W. H. AUDEN
Selected Poems

JANE AUSTEN
Emma
Mansfield Park
Northanger Abbey
Persuasion
Pride and Prejudice
Sense and Sensibility

HONORÉ DE BALZAC
Le Père Goriot

SAMUEL BECKETT
Waiting for Godot

SAUL BELLOW
Henderson, The Rain King

ARNOLD BENNETT
Anna of the Five Towns
The Card

WILLIAM BLAKE
Songs of Innocence, Songs of Experience

ROBERT BOLT
A Man For All Seasons

HAROLD BRIGHOUSE
Hobson's Choice

ANNE BRONTË
The Tenant of Wildfell Hall

CHARLOTTE BRONTË
Jane Eyre

EMILY BRONTË
Wuthering Heights

ROBERT BROWNING
Men and Women

JOHN BUCHAN
The Thirty-Nine Steps

JOHN BUNYAN
The Pilgrim's Progress

BYRON
Selected Poems

GEOFFREY CHAUCER
Prologue to the Canterbury Tales
The Clerk's Tale
The Franklin's Tale
The Knight's Tale
The Merchant's Tale
The Miller's Tale
The Nun's Priest's Tale
The Pardoner's Tale
The Wife of Bath's Tale
Troilus and Criseyde

SAMUEL TAYLOR COLERIDGE
Selected Poems

SIR ARTHUR CONAN DOYLE
The Hound of the Baskervilles

WILLIAM CONGREVE
The Way of the World

JOSEPH CONRAD
Heart of Darkness
Nostromo
Victory

STEPHEN CRANE
The Red Badge of Courage

BRUCE DAWE
Selected Poems

WALTER DE LA MARE
Selected Poems

DANIEL DEFOE
A Journal of the Plague Year
Moll Flanders
Robinson Crusoe

CHARLES DICKENS
A Tale of Two Cities
Bleak House
David Copperfield
Dombey and Son
Great Expectations
Hard Times
Little Dorrit
Oliver Twist
The Pickwick Papers

EMILY DICKINSON
Selected Poems

JOHN DONNE
Selected Poems

JOHN DRYDEN
Selected Poems

GERALD DURRELL
My Family and Other Animals

GEORGE ELIOT
Middlemarch
Silas Marner
The Mill on the Floss

T. S. ELIOT
Four Quartets
Murder in the Cathedral
Selected Poems
The Cocktail Party
The Waste Land

J. G. FARRELL
The Siege of Krishnapur

WILLIAM FAULKNER
Absalom, Absalom!
The Sound and the Fury

HENRY FIELDING
Joseph Andrews
Tom Jones

F. SCOTT FITZGERALD
Tender is the Night
The Great Gatsby

GUSTAVE FLAUBERT
Madame Bovary

E. M. FORSTER
A Passage to India
Howards End

JOHN FOWLES
The French Lieutenant's Woman

ATHOL FUGARD
Selected Plays

JOHN GALSWORTHY
Strife

MRS GASKELL
North and South

WILLIAM GOLDING
Lord of the Flies
The Spire

OLIVER GOLDSMITH
She Stoops to Conquer
The Vicar of Wakefield

ROBERT GRAVES
Goodbye to All That

GRAHAM GREENE
Brighton Rock
The Heart of the Matter
The Power and the Glory

WILLIS HALL
The Long and the Short and the Tall

THOMAS HARDY
Far from the Madding Crowd
Jude the Obscure
Selected Poems
Tess of the D'Urbervilles
The Mayor of Casterbridge
The Return of the Native
The Trumpet Major
The Woodlanders
Under the Greenwood Tree

L. P. HARTLEY
The Go-Between
The Shrimp and the Anemone

NATHANIEL HAWTHORNE
The Scarlet Letter

SEAMUS HEANEY
Selected Poems

JOSEPH HELLER
Catch-22

ERNEST HEMINGWAY
A Farewell to Arms
For Whom the Bell Tolls
The Old Man and the Sea

HERMANN HESSE
Steppenwolf

BARRY HINES
Kes

HOMER
The Iliad
The Odyssey

ANTHONY HOPE
The Prisoner of Zenda

GERARD MANLEY HOPKINS
Selected Poems

RICHARD HUGHES
A High Wind in Jamaica

TED HUGHES
Selected Poems

THOMAS HUGHES
Tom Brown's Schooldays

ALDOUS HUXLEY
Brave New World

HENRIK IBSEN
A Doll's House
Ghosts

HENRY JAMES
The Ambassadors
The Portrait of a Lady
Washington Square

SAMUEL JOHNSON
Rasselas

BEN JONSON
The Alchemist
Volpone

JAMES JOYCE
A Portrait of the Artist as a Young Man
Dubliners

JOHN KEATS
Selected Poems

PHILIP LARKIN
Selected Poems

D. H. LAWRENCE
Selected Short Stories
Sons and Lovers
The Rainbow
Women in Love

CAMARA LAYE
L'Enfant Noir

HARPER LEE
To Kill a Mocking-Bird

LAURIE LEE
Cider with Rosie

THOMAS MANN
Tonio Kröger

CHRISTOPHER MARLOWE
Doctor Faustus

ANDREW MARVELL
Selected Poems

W. SOMERSET MAUGHAM
Selected Short Stories

GAVIN MAXWELL
Ring of Bright Water

J. MEADE FALKNER
Moonfleet

HERMAN MELVILLE
Moby Dick

THOMAS MIDDLETON
Women Beware Women

THOMAS MIDDLETON and WILLIAM ROWLEY
The Changeling

ARTHUR MILLER
A View from the Bridge
Death of a Salesman
The Crucible

JOHN MILTON
Paradise Lost I & II
Paradise Lost IV & IX
Selected Poems

V. S. NAIPAUL
A House for Mr Biswas

ROBERT O'BRIEN
Z for Zachariah

SEAN O'CASEY
Juno and the Paycock

GABRIEL OKARA
The Voice

EUGENE O'NEILL
Mourning Becomes Electra

GEORGE ORWELL
Animal Farm
Nineteen Eighty-four

JOHN OSBORNE
Look Back in Anger

WILFRED OWEN
Selected Poems

ALAN PATON
Cry, The Beloved Country

THOMAS LOVE PEACOCK
Nightmare Abbey and *Crotchet Castle*

HAROLD PINTER
The Caretaker

SYLVIA PLATH
Selected Works

PLATO
The Republic

ALEXANDER POPE
Selected Poems

· York Notes: list of titles

J. B. PRIESTLEY
An Inspector Calls
THOMAS PYNCHON
The Crying of Lot 49
SIR WALTER SCOTT
Ivanhoe
Quentin Durward
The Heart of Midlothian
Waverley
PETER SHAFFER
The Royal Hunt of the Sun
WILLIAM SHAKESPEARE
A Midsummer Night's Dream
Antony and Cleopatra
As You Like It
Coriolanus
Cymbeline
Hamlet
Henry IV Part I
Henry IV Part II
Henry V
Julius Caesar
King Lear
Love's Labour's Lost
Macbeth
Measure for Measure
Much Ado About Nothing
Othello
Richard II
Richard III
Romeo and Juliet
Sonnets
The Merchant of Venice
The Taming of the Shrew
The Tempest
The Winter's Tale
Troilus and Cressida
Twelfth Night
GEORGE BERNARD SHAW
Androcles and the Lion
Arms and the Man
Caesar and Cleopatra
Candida
Major Barbara
Pygmalion
Saint Joan
The Devil's Disciple
MARY SHELLEY
Frankenstein
PERCY BYSSHE SHELLEY
Selected Poems
RICHARD BRINSLEY SHERIDAN
The School for Scandal
The Rivals
R. C. SHERRIFF
Journey's End
WOLE SOYINKA
The Road
EDMUND SPENSER
The Faerie Queene (Book I)
JOHN STEINBECK
Of Mice and Men
The Grapes of Wrath
The Pearl

LAURENCE STERNE
A Sentimental Journey
Tristram Shandy
ROBERT LOUIS STEVENSON
Kidnapped
Treasure Island
TOM STOPPARD
Professional Foul
Rosencrantz and Guildenstern are Dead
JONATHAN SWIFT
Gulliver's Travels
JOHN MILLINGTON SYNGE
The Playboy of the Western World
TENNYSON
Selected Poems
W. M. THACKERAY
Vanity Fair
DYLAN THOMAS
Under Milk Wood
FLORA THOMPSON
Lark Rise to Candleford
J. R. R. TOLKIEN
The Hobbit
ANTHONY TROLLOPE
Barchester Towers
MARK TWAIN
Huckleberry Finn
Tom Sawyer
JOHN VANBRUGH
The Relapse
VIRGIL
The Aeneid
VOLTAIRE
Candide
KEITH WATERHOUSE
Billy Liar
EVELYN WAUGH
Decline and Fall
JOHN WEBSTER
The Duchess of Malfi
H. G. WELLS
The History of Mr Polly
The Invisible Man
The War of the Worlds
OSCAR WILDE
The Importance of Being Earnest
THORNTON WILDER
Our Town
TENNESSEE WILLIAMS
The Glass Menagerie
VIRGINIA WOOLF
Mrs Dalloway
To the Lighthouse
WILLIAM WORDSWORTH
Selected Poems
WILLIAM WYCHERLEY
The Country Wife
W. B. YEATS
Selected Poems